Tsunami

WITPRESS

WIT Press publishes leading books in Science and Technology.
Visit our website for the current list of titles.
www.witpress.com

WITeLibrary

Home of the Transactions of the Wessex Institute, the WIT electronic-library provides the international scientific community with immediate and permanent access
to individual papers presented at WIT conferences.
Visit the WIT eLibrary athttp://library.witpress.com

Safety & Security Engineering Series

Series Editor: S. Mambretti, *Universidade Estadual de Campinas, Brasil*

Titles in Series

Flood Risk Assessment and Management
Landslides
Tsunami: From Fundamentals to Damage Mitigation

Tsunami

From Fundamentals to Damage Mitigation

Edited by

S. Mambretti

Universidade Estadual de Campinas, Brasil

Safety & Security Engineering Series

Series Editor: S. Mambretti, *Universidade Estadual de Campinas, Brasil*

Editor: S. Mambretti, *Universidade Estadual de Campinas, Brasil*

Published by

WIT Press

Ashurst Lodge, Ashurst, Southampton, SO40 7AA, UK
Tel: 44 (0) 238 029 3223; Fax: 44 (0) 238 029 2853
E-Mail: witpress@witpress.com
http://www.witpress.com

For USA, Canada and Mexico

WIT Press

25 Bridge Street, Billerica, MA 01821, USA
Tel: 978 667 5841; Fax: 978 667 7582
E-Mail: infousa@witpress.com
http://www.witpress.com

British Library Cataloguing-in-Publication Data

A Catalogue record for this book is available from the British Library

ISBN: 978-1-84564-770-4
eISBN: 978-1-84564-771-1
ISSN (print): 2047-7686
ISSN (online): 2047-7694

Library of Congress Catalog Card Number: 2012956053

The texts of the papers in this volume were set individually by the authors or under their supervision.

Contents

Preface ix

Chapter 1
Tsunami: from the open sea to the coastal zone and beyond 1
G. Mastronuzzi, H. Brückner, P.M. De Martini & H. Regnauld

1 Premise...1
2 Genesis of a tsunami 5
3 Evidence of the impacts of tsunami 9
   3.1 Offshore evidence 10
   3.2 Evidence on the coastal plain..14
   3.3 Evidence on the beach dune system 17
   3.4 Evidence on rocky coasts 20
4 Field evidence and risk assessment...23
Acknowledgments 26
References 27

Chapter 2
An inverse algorithm for reconstructing an initial Tsunami waveform 37
Tatyana Voronina

1 Introduction..37
2 Statement of the problem 42
3 Inverse method...44
4 *r*-solution...44
5 Discretization of the problem...45
6 Numerical experiments: description and discussion 48
7 Conclusion 54
Acknowledgements 56
References 56

Chapter 3
Tsunami maximum flooding assessment in GIS environment....................61
G. Mastronuzzi, S. Ferilli, A. Marsico, M. Milella, C. Pignatelli, A. Piscitelli,
P. Sansò & D. Capolongo

1 Introduction..61
2 Coastal geomorphology 64
3 Materials and methods 68

4 Tsunami height and manning number 70
5 The flooding area assessment 74
6 Discussion and conclusions 75
Acknowledgements 77
References 78

Chapter 4
Tsunami early warning coordination centres 81
J. Santos-Reyes & A.N. Beard

1 Introduction 81
2 A systemic disaster management system model 83
    2.1 The basic structural organization of the model 83
    2.2 System 2: early warning coordination centre 88
3 Modelling EWCC for the case of an Indian Ocean Country 88
4 Conclusions and future work 91
Acknowledgements 91
Annexure A 92
References 92

Chapter 5
RC buildings performance under the 2011 great East Japan Tsunami 95
C. Cuadra

1 Introduction 95
2 Characteristics of the earthquake and tsunami 96
    2.1 Tsunami source 96
3 Damages due to tsunami 100
    3.1 Selected area 100
    3.2 Damages on buildings 104
        3.2.1 Damages on wooden houses 104
        3.2.2 Damages on steel structures 105
        3.2.3 Damages on RC structures 107
4 Conclusions 109
References 109

Chapter 6
Infrastructure maintenance and disaster prevention measures on Islands:
example of the Izu Islands near Tokyo 111
H. Gotoh, M. Takezawa & T. Murata

1 Introduction 112
2 Outlines of Izu Islands 112
3 Population, aging, and industrial structures of Izu Islands 121
4 Land uses, infrastructures, and tourism of Izu Islands 123
5 Living standards and environmental hygiene in Izu Islands 128
6 Disaster prevention measures 129
7 Conclusions 137
References 137

Chapter 7
Health-related impacts of Tsunami disasters 139
Mark E. Keim

1 Background nature of tsunamis 139
   1.1 Definition 139
   1.2 Causes of tsunamis 140
   1.3 The physics of tsunami phenomenon 141
2 Scope and relative importance of tsunamis 142
3 Factors that contribute to the tsunami problem 144
4 Factors affecting tsunami occurrence and severity 144
5 Public health impact: historical perspective 145
6 Factors influencing mortality and morbidity 145
   6.1 Mortality trends 145
   6.2 Tsunami-associated illness and injury 146
   6.3 Infectious diseases 146
   6.4 Worsening of chronic diseases 148
   6.5 Psychosocial consequences 149
7 Conclusion 149
Disclaimer 150
References 150

Preface

In the last years the word "tsunami" has become familiar to most people, as many events have happened and drew the attention of both specialists and the general public because of their highly visible and spectacular actions and effects that have the potential to significantly affect society through loss of life, destruction of infrastructure and various other direct and indirect impacts.

Technically, a tsunami is a series of water waves caused by the displacement of a large volume of a body of water, typically in an ocean. Earthquakes, volcanic eruptions and other underwater explosions (including detonations of underwater nuclear devices), landslides, glacier calvings, meteorite impacts and other disturbances above or below water all have the potential to generate a tsunami.

Tsunami waves are very different from normal sea waves, because their wavelength is far longer. Wave heights of tens of metres can be generated by large events and therefore, although the impact of tsunamis is limited to coastal areas, their destructive power can be enormous and they can affect entire ocean basins; the 2004 Indian Ocean tsunami was among the deadliest natural disasters in human history with over 230,000 people killed in 14 countries bordering the Indian Ocean.

Scientists as well as governments must improve their grasp of knowledge regarding these natural hazards, as reducing the risks associated with them requires their better appreciation and understanding. This book comprises seven chapters, and covers all the main aspects related to tsunami.

The first chapter deals with the different types of tsunami and their historical data. Chapter 2 describes an inverse type solution to determine a posteriori of the tsunami waveform. One of the main problems with tsunamis is how to assess the flooding they produce, which is described in chapter 3.

Chapter 4 deals with the very important topic of Early Warning Systems. Chapter 5 not only studies the behaviour of reinforced concrete buildings under the 2011 Japanese Tsunami but puts forward a series of recommendations. One of the most damaging aspects of Tsunamis, is the damage to infrastructure and building systems, which is discussed in chapter 6, which also gives guideline measures to be taken in the future. Finally chapter 7 studies the important problem of health and related issues due to tsunami disasters.

The Editor is grateful to the Authors of these chapters, who are leading specialists in their fields and who prepared top quality material, that makes this volume a most valuable and up-to-date tool for professional, scientists and managers to appreciate the state-of-the-art in developing a fully integrated approach to tsunami risk management.

Stefano Mambretti
Brasil, 2013

CHAPTER 1

Tsunami: from the open sea to the coastal zone and beyond

G. Mastronuzzi[1], H. Brückner[2], P.M. De Martini[3] & H. Regnauld[4]
[1]*Dipartimento di Scienze della Terra e Geoambientali, Università degli Studi "Aldo Moro", Bari, Italy*
[2]*Geographisches Institut, Universität zu Köln, 50923 Köln (Cologne), Germany*
[3]*Istituto Nazionale di Geofisica e Vulcanologia, INGV, Roma, Italy*
[4]*Départment de Géographie, Université Rennes 2, Rennes, France*

Abstract

The impact of a tsunami is one of the most energetic phenomena that affects the Earth's surface, whether generated by earthquakes, submarine landslides, volcanic eruptions, meteorite impact or extreme weather conditions. As described in historical accounts or handed down orally from coastal populations that have been affected by this phenomenon, its remind is always connected to high waves advancing high-speed, flooding and destroying the coastal areas. On the following pages, the geomorphological effects of the flooding of coastal areas produced by historical and recent tsunamis are described. The study of coastal landscape and of the sediments recognizable along coastal plains, continental shelf, beaches and rocky coasts is tool that allows to reconstruct both the frequence of the phenomena and the capability to penetrate the coast and then to identify the limit of the maximum flooding. The knowledge derived from the study of their geomorphological evidence is essential for the definition of the concepts of hazard and vulnerability; these last are useful for the integrated coastal zone management and in the first aids planning.

1 Premise

The Chile tsunami[1] of February 27, 2010 (Magnitude: 8.8 Mw) occurred exactly 50 years after the destructive events of May 22, 1960 (seaquake and tsunami of

---

[1] "Tsunami" is a Japanese word, meaning "harbour wave." In Japanese, the plural is "tsunami" as well; the scientific literature often uses the plural form "tsunamis".

Figure 1: The memorial of the impact of the 1960 Chile tsunami along the
Japanese coasts in Matsubara Park at Minami – Sanriku, North Japan
before and immediately after the impact of the Tohoku-oki tsunami
(Photo: G. Mastronuzzi, April 12, 2011; K. Goto, April 2012).

Valdivia, Magnitude: 9.5 Mw); the impact of the Tohoku-oki tsunami on March
11, 2011 (M: 9.0 Mw) reminded the human coastal communities how their exposition to extreme waves is real and not just occasional (Fig. 1). During the last
20 years the Indo-Pacific region has been hit by an incredible sequence of strong
tsunamis that caused loss and damage to people, to human settlements, and to natural environments: Hokkaido 1993, Java 1999, Andaman 2004 (the Indian Ocean
Tsunami, IOT hereinafter), Java 2006, Samoa Islands 2009, Indonesia 2010, Chile
2010, Japan 2011 – all together these tsunamis killed at least 270,000 people along
the coasts of America, Asia and Africa, and induced invaluable damage. The transoceanic IOT, with its maximum run-up of 35 m and its counted 229,866 victims, is
considered to have caused one of the highest death tolls ever manifested in the history of the planet, being at the 13th/12th place in a terrifying list of killer 'natural'
disasters. The recent impact of strong tropical cyclones like Katrina (Louisiana,
2005), Sidr (Bangladesh, 2007) and Nargis (Myanmar, 2008) provoked rains, flash
floods and sea-flooding that caused about 140,000 fatalities.

Among others, both lists point out that these extreme events are even capable of
damaging technologically and socially advanced countries. Indeed, since tsunami
can occur by different causes, theoretically there is no coastal area in the world
that can be considered absolutely free from the possibility of the tsunami impact;
it can affect any coastal area of the planet with a minimum warning period [1, 2].
It is evident that the areas in which seismic and volcanic phenomena are active are
those in which the probability of a tsunami occurrence is higher.

The above-mentioned list could lead to the erroneous affirmation that tsunamis
occur only in the region with the highest seismicity in the world: the circum-pacific

'Ring of Fire'. Although the highest concentration of impact events known is actually around the Pacific Ocean, tsunamis are not only earthquake induced; in fact, the highest run-up (the maximum elevation reached by the tsunami wave) has been registered with 525 m above mean sea level in the narrow Lituya Bay, Alaska (July 9th, 1958) triggered by a large landslide as an effect of a failure of a mountain flank [3].

The impact of tsunami of regional interest is proven by legends and historical chronicles of many countries – from the Maori in New Zealand and the fishermen of the Karachi and Sendai regions, to the clericals of the Beauport Abbaye in Bretagne. Procopio da Cesarea (6th century AD) reported the effect of the quirks of Porfirione, the sea monster that generated waves capable to kill sailors and to destroy the coastal settlements in the Bosphorus area every 50 years (Guerra gotica, VII, 29). The Atlantis myth is frequently (but falsely) correlated to the destruction of the Minoan civilization as a consequence of the collapse of the Santorini volcano around 1620 BC and the subsequent tremendous tsunami that destroyed many ancient settlements in northern Crete (Fig. 2). Did it even cause the fast drop in sea level that favoured the exodus of the Israelites passing through the Red Sea (Exodus 14, 21–29)?

In connection with the availability of a long series of written documents, the Mediterranean peoples commemorate the occurrence of disastrous earthquakes that induced tsunami like the one of Crete in AD 365 that crossed the entire basin and destroyed Alexandria, Egypt, killing about 50,000 people (Ammiano Marcellino, Res Gestae, 26.10.15–19); the one that hit the coast of Israel, Palestine, Syria, Egypt, Turkey and Greece in AD 1303; the ones of eastern Sicily in AD 1169 and 1693, with about 20,000 and 60,000 victims, respectively. In more recent times the devastation induced by the maximum 13 m high run-up of the Reggio Calabria and Messina tsunami in AD 1908 was eyewitnessed by old men and women, still alive few years ago [4–6] (Fig. 3). One of the areas of the Mediterranean basin with the highest seismicity is the Aegean Sea; here in 1956 a strong earthquake generated a tsunami with a run-up of up to 20 m above sea level on the Amorgos Island [7].

Just outside the Mediterranean basin, the 'disaster of Lisbon' that took place on November 1, 1755, was generated by an earthquake that triggered a strong tsunami recorded all across the Atlantic Ocean: in Brazil, West Indies, France, Great Britain and Spain causing about 60,000 victims in Portugal, Spain and Morocco alone.

During the past few years, worldwide catalogues of tsunami events were elaborated [8–17]; they comprise far more than 2000 events during the past 4000 years, the biggest part of which has been identified mainly by means of historical and/or archaeological documentation. The importance of the geological imprint is generally underestimated [18] – even if this approach may furnish unique data on run-up heights and inundation distances for palaeo-tsunami events, contributing to the local hazard assessment. An immediate consequence is that only rarely the geologic record is used to calibrate probabilistic mathematical models of wave propagation.

Despite the fact that high-magnitude/low-frequency events are considered to have played an important role in the morphological evolution of many coastlines [1, 19],

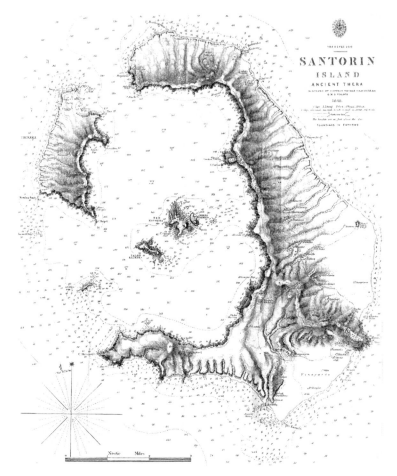

Figure 2: The caldera of Santorini Island (Greece) in a map drawn up by the Admiralty in 1848.

until recently even the scientific community has underestimated the importance of geomorphological and sedimentological criteria in the evaluation of the prediction of future scenarios, entrusting the assessment of the tsunami impact only to the geodynamic/mathematical models [20, 21]. They underrate the advantages derived from the study of field evidence to (*i*) individuate the areas hit by tsunami(s) in the past; (*ii*) set up a chronology of past events; (*iii*) validate with a deterministic approach the flooding models generally implemented only with mathematical models [22–25]. A multidisciplinary approach for the study of past and recent tsunami should not only involve geologists, geomorphologists, sedimentologists, palaeontologists, geochemists and geophysicists, but also engineers and biologists, archaeologists and historians, sociologists and economists; their cooperation in the Integrated Coastal Zone Management (ICZM) could make the impacts of possible future events less destructive.

Figure 3: Damage caused by the impact of the tsunami generated by the earthquake of December 8, 1908 in the port of Reggio Calabria, Italy (Alinavi, INGC-DPC).

2 Genesis of a tsunami

Even though our knowledge of tsunami generation is incomplete due to the lack of direct observation or measure of the triggering phenomena, commonly tsunamis are related to earthquakes/seaquakes, submarine or coastal landslides, turbidity flows, volcanic eruptions, specific meteorological conditions, meteorite impacts, etc. The generation mechanism of a tsunami is able to produce an abrupt and extensive disturbance of a big volume of water usually within oceans, seas or large lakes. Tsunamis have been reported since ancient times, especially in Japan and the Mediterranean, where long man-made records exist. Looking at the National Oceanic and Atmospheric Administration/World Data Center (NOAA/WDC) worldwide tsunami database spanning from 2000 BC to present (http://www.ngdc. noaa.gov/hazard/tsu.shtml) it is possible to find information on more than 2400 tsunami (Fig. 4).

In terms of global distribution the Pacific Ocean experienced about 63% of the total, while 21% occurred in the Mediterranean Sea, 6% in the Indian Ocean, and 5% in the Atlantic Ocean. Thus, the data suggest that tsunami could be generated everywhere and along every coastline; however, their distribution is mainly related to the position of plate boundaries and active volcanoes. In this sense, it is not a surprise to see how the 'Pacific Ring of Fire', a region well known for large earthquakes and significant volcanic activity, hosted more than half of the world-wide tsunami events while only a few tsunami were generated in the Atlantic Ocean, where there are no large subduction zones and passive continental margins instead. On the other hand, the most massive and destructive tsunami known, the IOT 2004, was generated in an area in which so far only the 6% of these event had been reported.

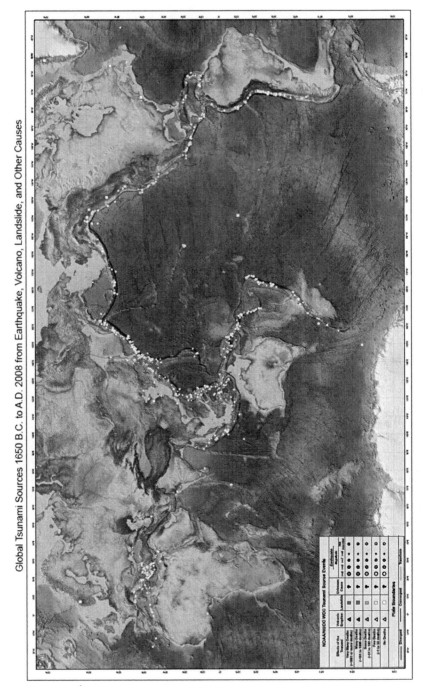

Figure 4: Distributions of tsunami around the world (http://www.ngdc.noaa.gov/hazard/tsu.shtml).

According to the NOAA/WDC database, most tsunamis are caused by earthquakes (73%) that are able to produce a rapid displacement of a large water column above the causative fault. Subduction zones are known to have been the loci of several tsunamigenic earthquakes since the 1960 Chile and 1964 Alaska events up to the recent 2004 Indian Ocean and 2011 Japan quakes, but significant tsunamis were generated also far from pure collision structures, like the 1755 Lisbon and the 1908 Messina Strait earthquakes.

The second tsunamigenic source type (5%) is related to the volcanic activity, both in terms of eruptions and collapses of all or part of the volcanic edifice. This mechanism is particularly efficient in rapidly transmitting a significant amount of energy to the nearby areas including oceans and seas. The 1620 BC Santorini volcano collapse and the August 27, 1883 Krakatoa eruption are known to have produced huge tsunami affecting the coastal communities at a regional scale, the latter one having killed about 40,000 persons.

Three to five per cent of the total number of tsunamis recorded in the NOAA worldwide database were generated by subaerial (coastal) and submarine landslides. A paradigmatic example can be the 1958 Lituya Bay (Alaska) landslide already mentioned earlier. More recently, a major instability event, deeply involving both the emerged and the submarine slope, occurred on the western flank of Stromboli volcano (Aeolian Islands, Italy), producing tsunami waves with a maximum run-up of over 10 m in the small coastal villages of Ficogrande and San Vincenzo. (Fig. 5).

Finally, among the most frequent sources we should mention the meteotsunamis that can account for up to 4% of the abovementioned database. They are known with different names: *rissaga* or *sexia* in the Balearic Islands (Spain), *marubbio* in Sicily, *milghuba* in Malta, *abiki* in the Nagasaki Bay (Japan) or *seebar* in the Baltic Sea. These events are related to specific meteorological conditions (deep depressions) able to generate storm surges. They can raise the tides up to several metres above the normal level, inundating large areas onshore. In the Adriatic Sea, on June 21, 1978 a perturbation travelling at speeds of about 22 m/s resulted in the flooding of the town of Vela Luka; in this case, the specific configuration of the coastline had amplified the phenomenon (Fig. 6).

Finally one should not forget the possibility of a meteorite impact into the ocean. The disappearance of the dinosaurs at the Cretaceous/Tertiary boundary some 65 Ma ago is hypothesized to have been a consequence of the impact of a great meteorite that triggered an impressive earthquake, dust dispersion with the consequence of a major climatic change and an impressive tsunami that flooded large parts of the emerged continental margins. Indeed, the impact of a meteorite is what can cause the most devastating effect because of its size and speed. Bryant (2001) assumes that meteorite-generated tsunami had hit the coast of Western Australia, the inundations of which reached some 10 km inland.

Finally, a curiosity: a man-induced tsunami occurred on December 6, 1917 in the city of Halifax (Nova Scotia, Canada) when a ship loaded with explosives exploded in the bay resulting in a disastrous giant sea level rise; the survivors witnessed three waves, one of which was more than 6 m high [26].

Figure 5: The Sciara del Fuoco at the flank of Stromboli (Aeolian Islands, Italy). The flank collapse on December 30, 2002 caused a tsunami with a run-up of up to 10 m (Photo INGV).

Figure 6: The flooding of Vela Luka (Korcula Island, former Yugoslavia) as consequence of the meteotsunami that occurred on June 21, 1978 (Archive of the City of Vela Luka).

3 Evidence of the impacts of tsunami

In general, the impact of an extremely strong wave, whatever its origin may be, can play an important role in the evolution of coastal areas [1, 27]. It can produce geomorphological and sedimentological evidence as a function of (*i*) the magnitude of the impacting energy; (*ii*) the morphotopographic features of the coasts; (*iii*) the lithostructural features of the coasts. Not all tsunamis are destructive, as low-energy tsunami cannot flood the coastal areas. But in the case of flooding, accumulation of a mixture of sediment and debris of marine and continental origin marks the inundated zone. Of course, these effects can be produced also by sea surges generated by exceptional sea storms with limited difference in extension in the case of flat coastal areas. The extreme waves can generate depositional (sandy/ muddy sheet, washover fan, isolated pebbles/boulders, sparse or arranged in berms, etc.) or erosive (platform, landslide, collision break, etc.) landforms at different scales, shaping typical 'high energetic' coastal 3D landscapes (e.g. [1, 28–47]).

The tsunami event can discharge its destructive energy to the coastal zone, triggering inundations that may reach many kilometres inland (Fig. 7). Despite the fact that during the last decade there was a rapid increase in the studies devoted to recognizing the fingerprints of past and recent tsunami impacts, there is still little

Figure 7: The Tohoku-oki tsunami flooded the coastal plain of Sendai. It reached all airport facilities built about 1.5 km from the shoreline (British News Agency The Daily Telegraph – http://savingjapan.net/).

agreement about what constitutes primary diagnostic criteria to distinguish storm from tsunami imprints. Megaboulders and coarse-clastic sediments in coastal environments have been largely considered indicative of the tsunami impact; sandy layers sandwiched in lacustrine or offshore sequences have been correlated with the transport of sandy beach sediments either inland by washover fans or seaward by the tsunami backwash. Recent studies performed in Italy, Netherland Antilles, France, Hawaii and Australia [41, 48–54] evidenced a series of features that can be explained by both tsunami and storm events.

The recent tsunami events have increased the attention to the geomorphological/ sedimentological evidence of their impact. The study of sediments and landforms associated with them should provide valuable information in the recognition on the past impacting wave characteristics, magnitude and frequency of marine flooding, and, consequently, on the assessment of potential future coastal hazard and risk scenarios.

Since there are many coasts that have been impacted in the past by large storm waves and/or by tsunamis, it is important to develop criteria to distinguish between the two types of events (Fig. 8). In the following, the depositional evidence of tsunami impacts is described.

3.1 Offshore evidence

To date, the international scientific community does not have a commonly accepted set of approaches to be adopted for the identification and characterization of tsunami deposits in the marine realm. This is mainly due to the very limited

Figure 8: View of the Sendai coastal plain. On the right the core GPS 505 in which an 'out of place' layer connected to the Jogan tsunami (AD 869) was recognized (Photo: G. Mastronuzzi, April 11, 2010).

number of offshore studies on this subject. Only in recent years, research started to investigate the offshore more closely looking for tsunami signatures, thanks to the large amount of data collected after the 2004 IOT and the 2011 Japan tsunami. As for the IOT, both inflow (landward) and outflow (seaward) had produced intense erosion, sediment transport and deposition (from fine sand to boulder) up to about 5 km inland and about 2.5 km offshore [55]. Moreover, during the IOT the amount of sediments reworked, transported and deposited offshore was significant; it was probably larger than the volume deposited inland [55]. These recent studies should be taken into consideration by the international community in order to develop specific projects for the tsunamis research offshore. In fact, the marine realm is potentially more sensitive to 'anomalous' events (i.e., not only tsunamis but also earthquakes) than the coastal environments – where fingerprints may get lost due to erosion and bioturbation – and may provide relatively undisturbed and continuous sedimentary records, if they are not lost due to bioturbation. As already mentioned, only a few cases are available and all tend to adopt a multiproxy approach.

In order to sketch a preliminary set of evidences for the identification and characterization of tsunami signatures offshore, several interesting studies are presented in the following, moving from the abyssal plain to the nearshore.

In order to investigate great magnitude tsunamigenic events, such as the c. 1620 BC Santorini collapse and the AD 1755 Lisbon earthquake, the study of abyssal plain turbidite deposits was found to be a promising element.

Cita and Aloisi [56] detected a megaturbidite (up to 30 m thick) on the Ionian and Syrte abyssal plains and studied it mainly using geophysical and sedimentological tools. A three-dimensional reconstruction is the essence of their paper, suggesting that the megaturbidite was deposited as a result of huge tsunami waves. In fact, the authors hypothesize that tsunami waves, likely related to the Late Bronze Age Santorini event, may have induced pressure pulses and near-bottom currents strong enough to mobilize unconsolidated sediments of the inner shelf, producing turbidite flows that spread over a wide deep area like the Ionian and Syrte abyssal plains (Fig. 9).

Gràcia et al. [57] applied the 'turbidite paleoseismology' concept to the SW Iberian margin and found that, apart from specific climatic events, earthquakes and tsunamis are the most likely triggering mechanism for synchronous, widely distributed turbidites in the area of study.

The analysis of several sediment cores retrieved from four different abyssal plains of the SW Iberian margin highlighted the presence of an important turbidite. Several multidisciplinary analyses (from physical properties to geochemical proxies) provide evidence for seven widespread megaturbidites. ^{210}Pb, ^{137}Cs and ^{14}C dating provided ages that correlate with the dates of important instrumentally and historically recorded tsunamigenic earthquakes (e.g., the 1969 and 1755 events); thus, a Holocene tsunami recurrence interval of about 1800 years could be calculated [57]. A further element in favour of a tsunami origin derived from the positive correlation between the ages of two turbidites (AD 1755 and 218 BC) with the ages of two tsunami deposits found on land along the shores of the Gulf of Cadiz [58].

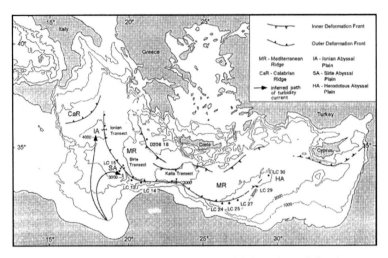

Figure 9: Sketch of the Mediterranean basin with location of the deep-sea core in the base of which the megaturbidite was detected. It was presumably triggered by the tsunami hitting the shoreline of the Syrte Gulf which was generated by the Santorini eruption [56].

Moving from the deep abyssal basins to the continental shelf, Smedile *et al.* [59, 60] recently presented a study carried out on a 6.7 m long, fine sediment core sampled at a water depth of 72 m, 2.3 km offshore the Augusta bay (Eastern Sicily). Research involving X-ray imaging, high-resolution measurement of physical properties, grain-size analysis, micropaleontology, isotopic dating methods (^{210}Pb, ^{137}Cs and ^{14}C) and tephrochronology were carried out, looking for any subtle anomaly that could represent a proxy for tsunami occurrence. The first interesting evidence was the presence of 12 anomalous layers, marked by a high concentration of displaced epiphytic foraminifera, as highlighted by a multivariate analysis on benthic foraminiferal assemblages (Fig. 10).

Minor grain-size changes and peculiar bimodal particle-size distribution were found to characterize these layers. Smedile *et al.* [59] suggest that these 12 layers could be related to high-energy tsunami backwash waves able to disperse an important quantity of infralittoral epiphytic species from the nearshore (they may live up to a maximum water depth of 35 m) towards deeper areas (outer shelf). The proposed tsunami mechanism is also supported by the matching between historical tsunami accounts, both local and basin-wide ones (those of AD 1908, 1693, 1169, 365 Crete and the ≈3.6 ka B.P. Santorini tsunami), and the age windows of five studied layers. Moreover, the ages of seven events identified in the offshore sediments show a positive correlation with the ages of tsunami deposits found onshore along the Augusta Bay coastline [61], reinforcing the tsunami mechanism hypothesis.

Another interesting approach was tested offshore Caesarea (Israel) by Goodman-Tchernov *et al.* [62]. The authors studied four sediment cores collected on the

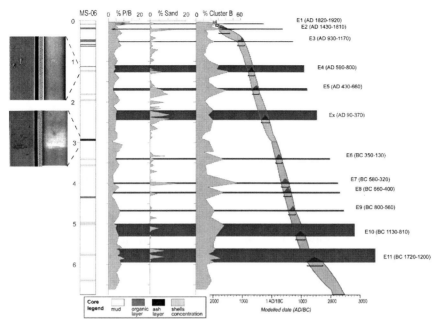

Figure 10: The MS-06 core log together with plankton and benthos ratios (% P/B), sand distribution (% Sand) and concentration of epiphytic displaced species (% Cluster B). The grey horizontal bands highlight the 12 intervals of positive correlations between sedimentological and foraminiferal characteristics. On the left side details of sediments and X-ray showing a shell concentration layer and the tephra level. On the right part of the figure, the age/depth model, built on the basis of a P sequence from OxCal 4.1 software with the probability distribution ranges (2σ). The change in colour of the age/depth model represents a strong boundary change inserted in coincidence of the Etna tephra (122 BC). The 12 layers are dated following this age/depth model, assuming the age of the deposit at the base of each of them as the closest to the beginning of the exceptional high-energy episode (modified after [60]).

upper continental shelf (maximum water depth: 20 m). It should be noted that, because of the difficulty in differentiating tsunamigenic layers from deposits caused by storms or fluvial flooding in the nearshore zone, upper shelf tsunami deposits are very rare in the international literature. The pluridisciplinary approach consisted mainly of grain-size analysis, micropalaeontology and archaeology. The authors used detailed analysis of the particle-size distribution to identify, differentiate and characterize tsunami and storm deposits. Archaeological estimates on pottery fragments were combined with several radiocarbon and OSL age estimates in order to establish a precise chronology. Three horizons showing tsunamigenic indicators are tentatively associated with historical events from Roman and Byzantine times, as well as the Santorini eruption (≈1620 BC).

3.2 Evidence on the coastal plain

The effect of tsunami waves on coasts is that by such an extreme event the coast-lines and coastal areas may be changed dramatically within a few hours only. Often the transformation is both erosive and accumulative. At Cape Pakarang, Thailand, this was clearly evidenced by the impact of the IOT on December 26, 2004. The comparison of the before and after satellite images and photographs shows, on the one hand, the total erosion of the sandy cape and the estuary-like widening of the river mouths, the latter having been caused mainly by the back-flowing water masses, which – other than the incoming tsunami wave train – are channelled (Fig. 11). On the other hand, the transport and deposition of big boulders on the reef platform demonstrates the accumulation part of the event (Fig. 12).

Among the most startling discoveries in sedimentology in the last decades were sand layers in coastal peats or mires that could be traced back to tsunami impact: a famous example is that of Washington State, where Atwater [63] found a stratum of marine sand that had been deposited by the Alaska 1964 tsunami. Another famous example comes from the Scottish moors, where littoral fine sediment is sandwiched between peat strata; the reason was the Storegga tsunami, caused by a failure of the continental slope of the Norwegian Trench [19, 64–67].

Swales between beach ridges are another interesting geomorphological feature for archiving the sedimentary footprint of a tsunami. On Phra Thong Island, a backhoe trench revealed several tsunamites, embedded in peaty material (Fig. 13).

While the event layer can be dated directly with the luminescence (age of depo-sition) and possibly with the ^{14}C (age of tsunami-transported macro-remains) dat-ing techniques, the surrounding peat can be dated with ^{14}C; the synopsis of the three ages will give the best estimate for the age of the tsunami. Through the long extension of the trench it became also evident that the predecessors of the IOT

Figure 11: River mouth at Ban Bang Sak, Thailand after the IOT. The lower course of the river was widened as an effect of the back flowing waters after inundation. After the event, the beach has partly recovered (sand bar in front) (Photo: H. Brückner, March 3, 2010).

2004 are not fully recorded everywhere; in fact, a drilling at one site might trace only the IOT, at another site it may additionally reveal 2–3 palaeo-tsunamites.

On the island of Bonaire (Leeward Antilles), a palaeo-tsunamis chronology was established using radiocarbon-dated overwash deposits. They were identified in sediment cores from floodplains and lagoonal shores bearing sedimentary character-istics typically found in cases of modern tsunami. Uncertainties in sediment inter-pretation associated with the fact that most of these tsunami signature types may also occur in storm deposits, were reduced based on (*i*) the high tsunami potential of the southern Caribbean with several potential triggering mechanisms; (*ii*) the

Figure 12: Boulder field at Cape Pakarang, Thailand. The boulders appeared on the reef platform as an effect of the Indian Ocean Tsuami of December 26, 2004 (IOT) (Photo: H. Brückner, November 18, 2008).

Figure 13: Backhoe trench on Phra Thong Island showing the deposits of the IOT 2004 (uppermost layer of grey sand), and of its predecessor (light grey layer), sandwiched between two peat strata. The latter event occurred ca. 400–600 years ago (Photo: H. Brückner, March 5, 2010).

identification of sediment source areas which are out of reach for storm waves; (*iii*) the lack of littoral and marine sand/mud input during recent high-category hurricanes [68]. Whereas deposition of these layers by extraordinary tropical cyclones (the energy of which should have significantly exceeded the one of the most severe ones the island has witnessed in historical times) is unlikely, the tsunami hypothesis is also fuelled by local investigations on the coarse-clast record [69–71] (Fig. 14).

In NW Greece, repeated tsunamis impact on the coastal zone between Lefkada and Preveza was inferred based on sedimentary and geomorphological findings. Here, allochthonous sand and shell debris layers of marine origin intercalated within the lagoonal sedimentary sequence of the Lefkada Sound were interpreted as tsunami deposits [72]. Washover structures stretching into in the Lefkada Lagoon corroborate these findings since they are considered as geomorphological remains of severe tsunami inundation, due to their distinct sedimentary characteristics, their stratigraphical architecture and the relatively low impact of modern storms on the back-barrier geomorphology (Fig. 15).

Figure 14: Vibracoring in the silted up landward part of the bay of Boka Washikemba, Bonaire, Leeward Antilles (Photo: C. Pignatelli, March 9, 2006).

Figure 15: Washover structures stretching into in the Lefkada Lagoon, Ionian Islands, Greece (Photo: G. Mastronuzzi, September 29, 2008).

In the given case the washover fans are suggested to have formed during Classical-Hellenistic times [35], and by the tsunami following the AD 365 Crete earthquake [73] that severely affected coastlines of the entire central-eastern Mediterranean [20, 74]. Several coarse clastic sediment layers traced in Lake Voulkaria [35, 37, 38] and in sedimentary archives of the adjacent coastal area were interpreted to be of tsunamigenic origin as well [75, 76]. Based on these findings, May *et al.* [77] concluded that tsunami events significantly influenced the Holocene coastal evolution in the Lefkada–Preveza area.

3.3 Evidence on the beach dune system

Tsunamis have tremendous impacts on beaches; however, since the beach is a very resilient feature, they are not long-lasting ones. On dunes, however, the impacts are less destructive, but may last longer and may be used to date the occurrence of the event. When the tsunami waves hit the beach, they have two main effects: on the one hand they bring material to the beach, on the other they take material from the beach and move it landward first (run-up phase), and seaward later (backwash phase). These two effects may happen together or may be separated in time.

Most of the material brought to the beach had been eroded from the near-by sea floor; it may range in size from sand to boulder. This input may raise the beach profile, at least temporarily, and change the beach response to the next wave(s). As a rule, the imported sediment is coarser than the local one as tsunami waves have much more energy than ordinary storm waves (though some exceptional storms may also bring very coarse material and even boulders [78]). It is, therefore, very difficult to sort out the exact origin of a coarse layer in a beach setting. For example, the presence of beached remains of entire cetaceans along the coast of Miramar Peninsula, Wellington, New Zealand is a possible evidence of the impact of historical tsunami [79].

When the tsunami waves hit the beach profile, the sand is put in suspension and moves landward with the water. This means there is a net loss of original material (the sediment that was there before the tsunami) in the beach system. This loss may or may not be compensated by the material brought in by the waves. There is no clear general explanation that would help to understand why in some cases the gain and loss are balanced whereas in other cases erosion or deposition dominates. It seems that this behaviour is very much dependant on the local coastal configuration, and that the foreshore topography plays an important role. When the water begins to move seaward during the start of the backwash phase at the end of the tsunami peak inundation, large eddies may form and erode the beach, transporting material seaward. This was studied in Tierra del Fuego by Bujalesky [80]: in the Ensenada de la Colonia embayment, a large regressive beach ridge plain composed of gravel and coarse sand had been impacted by at least three waves of a single tsunami. The result was a net loss and an export of gravel and sand seaward leading to the formation of semicircular erosive scarps. Moreover, the landform analysis suggests a sequence of three to five landward overwashing and overtopping events. The semicircular erosive scarps and the overtopping fans were created by tsunami that had reached the Atlantic coast of Tierra del Fuego.

On the other hand the impact of a tsunami can cause a beach growth. This occurred during the strong 1854 Ansei-Tokai earthquake that triggered a large scale tsunami that hit Suruga Bay, central Japan. There waves of about 13 m height struck Iruma at its southeastern coast where a huge mound of shoreface sand, reaching more than 11.2 m above the sea level, appeared after the tsunami run-up. Sedimentological survey and submarine investigation brought to light that the sand came from the foreshore seafloor with water depths of 20 to 30 m. Moreover, historical data highlighted that the tsunami run-up was responsible for a dramatic change of the landform, generating a large sandy dome [81]. Impacts of tsunami on dunes are relatively well understood as they have been studied in several countries [82]. The tsunami impacts the fore-dunes (and may partly destroy them), and the water runs up the main dune slope. It acts as a blade, eroding a thin sheet of surficial sand from the dune's sea facing slope, and depositing it on the top or on the landward side of the dune. In this respect, the tsunami waves act exactly as a storm surge. In New Zealand a tsunami hit a large set of beaches (minimum age of 1180–930 cal BP in Henderson Bay; [40]), and deposited a sheet of gravel taken from the sea floor on top of the dunes. In the Falkland Islands, another tsunami topped the dunes with a sheet of marine gravels [42] (Figs. 16 and 17).

It is obvious that tsunami waves not only have sea water but do contain large objects (e.g. the ones taken from the nearby seafloor). These objects may hit the dune slope, creating a definite but very localized erosive effect. In Henderson Bay, a gully was locally carved within the dune face by the tsunami, destroying some Maori cooking places. Today, this gully is still active [40].

The high capacity of a tsunami to destroy the beach system has been underlined by some studies performed in the Mediterranean basin, like the above mentioned

Figure 16: Oblique air photo of Pebble Island (Falkland Archipelago). This part of the coast has been hit by a tsunami which has first eroded the thin preexisting soil and deposited a sheet of gravel on top of a former dune field. Part of it is being re-colonised by vegetation, the other part is used as a nursery for gentoos (*Pygoscelis papua*) (Photo: H. Regnauld, January, 2006).

in the area of Lefkada and Preveza, NW Greece. In northern Apulia, the Lesina Lake is closed by a polyphasic dune ridge [30, 31]. A sequence of four tsunami occurred in the fifth century BC, on AD 493, 1087 and 1627. In this case, the impacting waves crossed the dune ridge in the area in which earthquakes had generated fractures in the local clay basement, depositing huge washover fans in the lake (Fig. 18).

The backwash accumulated seaward large quantities of sand with which later the dune ridge was reconstructed and the erosive gaps were filled. Not far from the lake, the delta of the Fortore River was eroded by the backwash effect. In this case study as well, despite the high energy of the impacting waves, the presence of sediments inland is not extensive but limited to some depressions up to 1 km inland – the best traps for tsunami sediments – as evidenced by De Martini *et al.* [32] who detected

Figure 17: Ground photo of the gravel sheet, where vegetation is beginning to grow again on a new soil (Pebble Island, Falkland Archipelago) (Photo: H. Regnauld, January, 2006).

Figure 18: Aerial view of the Lesina Lake coastal barrier and of the Foce Cauto fan; the excavation of pools for shrimp farming determined the strong reworking of the sediments (Photo: M. Caldara, Bari, Italy).

in several cores only some decimetres of deposits (up to 15 cm) and even without a characteristic marine imprint.

In the cases aforementioned, the geomorphological effect of the tsunami impact is more evident than the sedimentological one. The erosion of the beach ridges and the accumulation of the washover fans are more obvious than the sediment accumulation inland, mainly represented by thin sand deposits no more than some decimetres thick. A large part of the sand moved seaward due to backwash. As evidenced by studies of the sediment transported inland by the Tohoku-oki tsunami in the Sendai plain, sediments do not always show well-recognizable marine characteristics since they are a mixture of onshore and offshore sands associated with soil debris [83, 84]. Even the largest tsunami may not transport large quantities of marine sediments on land. Like in the case of rocky coasts or coastal plains, tsunami impacts on beaches and dunes are highly variable and may range from deposition to erosion, according to very local conditions. A lot of field work still has to be done before scientists may understand clearly the beach response to such extreme events. This has been exemplified by several colleagues for the March 11, 2011 Tohoku-oki tsunami (e.g. [85]; see also the whole issue of *Sedimentary Geology*).

3.4 Evidence on rocky coasts

Field study performed all along the coasts of the world permitted to recognize the presence of megaboulders, isolated and sparse or arranged in fields or berms in the intertidal/littoral zone, accumulated along the rocky coasts and in protected areas of coral reefs. They represent the most impressive evidence of the impact of extreme waves. These frequent morphological features have been attributed to the impact of extreme waves that had occurred in the past or were evidenced by post-event surveys ([86–88] for Japan; [89] for Thailand; [90] for the Cayman Islands; [28, 91, 92] for the southeastern coast of Australia; [93] for the Bahamas; [94] for Spain; [29, 39, 48, 95] for Italy; [33–35, 37, 96, 97] for Cyprus and Greece).

Not always does the presence of these unusual landforms find the agreement of the scientists concerning their shaping event. Historic tsunamis are known to have transported and deposited large boulders [55, 89, 98]. Furthermore, studies of palaeotsunami have also reported the deposition of boulders as isolated clasts or stacked/imbricated clusters [99, 100]. However, in the absence of direct eyewitnesses, the finding of boulders still pose the question: Are they the effect of a palaeo-storm (tempestite) or a palaeo-tsunami (tsunamite)? In some cases, there is evidence that boulder emplacement can be produced by severe storms or hurricanes [48, 51, 101–103]. Yet in recent studies, different authors underlined the fact that storms and tsunamis can generate phenomena of morphologic convergence concerning coastal features [48, 69, 101, 102, 104, 107]. Indeed, storms and tsunamis can scatter boulders inland and accumulate them in emerged coastal areas as a function of the dissipation of their energy as well as the coastal bathymetry and topography. Generally, boulder weighing up to some tens of tons are arranged in fields and are locally imbricated; in some cases they show a lateral sorting with the biggest and heaviest being close to the coastline and the smallest being far inland. In other cases, hundreds of boulders are arranged in berms in a chaotic distribution. Their extensive presence contributes to identify the sequence of past tsunamis also along rocky coasts in which other fingerprints are not recognizable. The capacity to reconstruct the occurrence of past tsunamis impact from boulder fields may help in the assessment of the effects of impacts in the future [46, 108, 109].

It may well be that dislocated big boulders on gently sloping rocky coasts can be considered as the strongest evidence for the impact of tsunami waves. Kelletat and Schellmann [96] described boulder fields on Cyprus, which they interpret as tsunamigenic; Scheffers [69] mapped coral boulders on Bonaire in the Caribbean. However, this kind of evidence has been challenged, when the origin of the boulder dislocation was interpreted as the effect of storm waves [110]. The dispute can be settled by considering laws of physics when it comes to calculating the energy needed for a boulder of a given size and density to be dislocated from the cliff for a certain distance inland and uphill. Lately Benner *et al.* [111] and Engel and May [71] have done so and roughly determined the maximum threshold concerning the transport and uplift capacities of a storm. Thus, the authors can prove that even a very severe storm (hurricane category 5+) cannot have transported some of the megaboulders on Bonaire (Fig. 19).

In this context, the most impressive evidence is known from the Ishikagi Island, Prefecture of Okinawa, Japan where a calcarenite boulder weighing 200 t was dislocated up to 10 m above sea level 100 m inland by the Okinawa-Sakishima tsunami about 2000 yr BP [112] (Fig. 20). In the Miyara Bay, a field of giant boulders up to 600 t was deposited by the 1771 Meiwa tsunami; the same holds true for the Ibaruma coast where in an extended boulder field the biggest boulder among the tsunami deposits is made up of a single coral colony [88, 113–115] (Fig. 21).

Figure 19:   Megaboulder on Bonaire, Leeward Antilles. The boulder broke into two pieces when it was deposited on the Last Interglacial reef platform after having been dislocated from the cliff by a tsunami impact (Photo: H. Brückner, July 16, 2011).

Figure 20: The 'tsunami ufu-ishi', a coralline boulder ($13 \times 12 \times 7.5$ m^3), deposited by the 1771 Meiwa tsunami on the Southern coast of the Ishigaki
Island, Okinawa, Japan; it is placed at 10 m above the present mean sea
level and about 100 m inland (Photo: G. Mastronuzzi, April 14, 2010).

Figure 21: The 'Bari-ishi' (split boulder in Japanese), a 216 tons heavy coralline
boulder dislocated from the reef by the 1771 Meiwa tsunami (Ibaruma
coast, Ishikagi Island, Okinawa, Japan) (Photo: G. Mastronuzzi, April
14, 2010).

Megaboulders attributed to the impact of tsunami have been recognized not
only in the Indian and Pacific Oceans, but also all along the coasts of the Mediterranean Sea [116]. For example, along the Otranto–Leuca coast near Torre
Sant'Emiliano (SE Apulia, Italy), an impressive arrangement of large boulders
was studied. It is about 30 m wide and follows the present coastline for about
2.5 km at a varying distance of 15 to 40 m. Looking closer, it is composed of two
ridges. Its top reaches about 11 m above mean sea level. Huge blocks, weighing up
to 70 t, cover the carved surface stretching from the coastline to the front of the

Figure 22: The impressive 2.5 km long boulders berms put in place by the February 20, 1743 tsunami at Torre Sant'Emiliano (Otranto, Lecce, Italy). The berms are placed up to 10 m above m.s.l. and 60 m inland, the boulder are up to 70 tons heavy (Photo: P. Sansò, July 21, 2006).

first ridge (Fig. 22). AMS-^{14}C age estimates performed on marine shells found the boulders to have been accumulated recently, i.e., within the last three centuries. Moreover, archaeological remains in the top layers of the colluvial deposits covered by the boulders date from the 16th/17th century.

This evidence suggests that the February 20, 1743 earthquake was responsible for the generation of two large tsunami waves that caused the boulder displacement. This quake was particularly violent in the Salento region where it reached grade IX on the MCS scale. Interestingly, chronicles of this event record a withdrawal of the sea in the harbour of Brindisi north of the study area [39].

4 Field evidence and risk assessment

The increasing human activity in coastal areas all over the world makes these landscapes vulnerable to the occurrence of extreme events with great impact like tsunamis and exceptional storm surges. In a context of global change, storms are not any more events localized in some tropical and high latitude areas; in the Mediterranean an increase of extreme meteorological events has been registered in the past few decades [117–119]. On the other hand, the propagation of a tsunami can gain a transoceanic importance as evidenced by the recent events IOT 2004, Chile 2010 and Japan 2011 (Fig. 23).

Different geodynamic, geological and geomorphological features of the sea bottom and of the coastal area together define the hazard, vulnerability and, consequently, risk as a function of the coastal value (e.g. [120–122]). These phenomena are rarely taken into account by planners, with the exception of circum-pacific

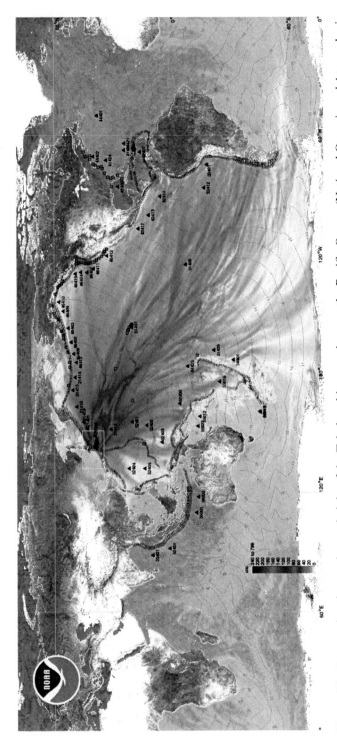

Figure 23:   Propagation time and wave height of the Tohoku-oki tsunami across the Pacific Ocean. (National Oceanic and Atmospheric Administration; http://nctr.pmel.noaa.gov/honshu20110311/honshu2011-globalmaxplot.png; March 2011).

areas where the high frequency and intensity of tsunamis have imposed the real-ization of structures and procedures for the mitigation of the risk.

First of all, the geological records can identify areas that have a (high) potential for being affected by new events; they may be less energetic, however, more destructive. The presence of deposits and landforms, if accurately dated by radio-metric methods, archaeological and historical data, allows to recognize the sequence of the events and, as a consequence, the assessment of the hazard. Unfor-tunately, given the nature of tsunamis, a probabilistic approach on a significant number of events should be adopted in order to use their geomorphological evi-dence to define the return time. The innermost limit of the geological evidence must be used to evaluate the flooding limit due to past tsunami impact. The inte-gration of geological and hydrodynamic data with geophysical and mathematical models can allow for an estimation of the water level during the tsunami event responsible for boulder transport. Moreover, it should be possible to calculate how far the impacting wave will extend inland in case of a new event; this is a function of the wave parameters and of the degree of roughness of the flooded terrain. Recent hydrodynamic theories tried to put in relation sediment features and/or boulders sizes, and coastal features to the wave responsible for their accumulation, developing mathematical formulas. The sandy deposits have been used to evaluate the tsunami flow speed [123–125]. Jonathan Nott introduced a numerical approach that enables the reconstruction of wave heights of tsunami and storm waves neces-sary to transport certain coastal boulders. This approach mainly relies on the bal-ance of cumulated uplifting and restraining forces as well as a relationship between overland flow velocity and wave height [126, 127]. The hypothesis is that starting from the boulder size and shape and knowing the local wave climate, it should be possible to discriminate between storm and tsunami inland scattering [24, 25, 50, 70, 126, 129, 130]. These equations have experienced modifications and improve-ments step by step [25, 111, 131].

Recently, Marsico et al. [132], Pignatelli et al. [70, 130], Mastronuzzi and Pig-natelli [133], Engel and May [71] and Hoffmeister et al. [134] pointed to the importance of reliable data for boulder volume by Terrestrial Laser Scanning, DGPS, LiDAR or photogrammetry if Nott-type equations are applied. Going back to the example of Bonaire (Leeward Antilles) once more: there the largest coastal blocks were investigated as potential evidence for the occurrence of more power-ful waves than those of the strongest tropical cyclones in the region. By comparing calculated minimum storm wave heights required to quarry and move the largest blocks of the boulder fields of NE Bonaire with maximum wave heights observed during recent high-category hurricanes and the buoy record, little doubt remains that one or more major tsunamis happened in the Mid- to Late Holocene, even though local observations on tsunamis occurrence are lacking for historical times [70, 71]. The use of hydrodynamic equations and/or mathematical models (e.g. [89, 127, 128, 135, 136] in relation to the coastal morphology, allows for the mod-elling of the maximum flooding and of the risk assessment [121, 130].

For the southern Adriatic and Ionian coasts, the available tsunamis data set points out a recurrence period of about 25/50 years with a maximum intensity of

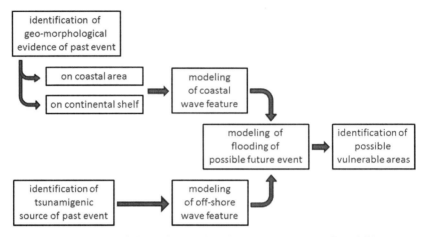

Figure 24: Flowchart of the actions to be taken to assess the vulnerability respect
to the possible occurrence of a tsunami.

III–VI degree (Ambraseys-Sieberg scale) [8]. The new morphological data are
related to tsunamis that hit the central Mediterranean area within the last three mil-
lennia. Unluckily, available data along the rocky coasts are restricted to the past
few centuries, since recent tsunamis could have modified or erased the effects of
older ones [48, 121].

However, the available data set stresses the fact that the hazard due to tsunami
impact is not negligible and that geological data along with historical accounts
allow for a well-based risk assessment. This is of fundamental importance for the
planning of civil protection measures. The integration of hazard and vulnerability
data arranged in a GIS will define the Land Use Capability, needed for the correct
planning of coastal areas. It is our conviction that science should improve the
methodologies used in the study of the tsunami deposits also for the knowledge
about their possible impact in a scenario characterized by the rapid and uncon-
trolled presence of human settlements along the coasts of highly vulnerable areas.
As scientists we strongly believe that our disciplines should (*i*) improve their
methods of studying past tsunami deposits and of mapping their extension, and
(*ii*) in agreement with the obtained results build scenarios for the forecast of future
impacts (Fig. 24).

The occurrence of the IOT and the Japan tsunamis drastically underlined the
necessity for an Integrated Coastal Zone Management (ICZM) that integrates the
knowledge about the tsunami danger as well, with respect to magnitude and frequency of these catastrophic events.

Acknowledgments

The paper is a French-German-Italian contribution to the   project IGCP 588 –
International Geological Correlation Programme "Preparing for coastal change.

A detailed response process framework for coastal change at different times" by UNESCO – IUGS ((project Leaders: Dr. Adam D. Switzer, Earth Observatory of Singapore (EOS), Nanyang Technological University, Dr. Craig Sloss, School of Natural resources Sciences, Queensland University of Technology, Australia, Dr. Benjamin Horton, Department of Earth and Environmental Sciences, University of Pennsylvania, Dr. Yongqiang Zong, Department of Earth Sciences, University of Hong Kong, China).

Researches have been supported by funds managed by each Author, and also by the Research Unit of the University of Bari (resp. Prof. G. Mastronuzzi) as part of the Italian Project RITMARE.

References

[1] Bryant, E.A., *Tsunami. The Underrated Hazard.* Cambridge University Press: Cambridge, UK, 2001.

[2] Morner, N.-A. (ed), *The Tsunami Threat: Research And Technology.* INTECH: Croatia, 2011.

[3] Mader, C.L., Modeling the 1958 Lituya Bay Mega-Tsunami. *Science of Tsunami Hazards*, **17**, pp. 57–67, 1999.

[4] Piatanesi, A. & Tinti, S., A revision of the eastern Sicily earthquake and tsunami. *Journal of Geophysical Research*, **103**, pp. 2749–2758, 1998.

[5] Tinti, S. & Guiliani, D., The Messina Straits tsunami of December 28, 1908: a critical review of experimental data and observations. *Il Nuovo Cimento*, **60(4)**, pp. 429–442, 1983.

[6] Tinti, S. & Armigliato, A., The use of scenarios to evaluate tsunami impact in South Italy. *Marine Geology*, **199(3–4)**, pp. 221–243, 2003.

[7] Okal, E.A., Synolakis, C.E., Uslu, B., Kalligeris, N. & Voukouvalas, E., The 1956 earthquake and tsunami in Amorgos, Greece. *Geophysics Journal International*, **178**, pp. 1533–1554, 2009.

[8] Soloviev, S.L., Solovieva, O.N., Go, C.N., Kim, K.S. & Shchetnikov, N.A., Tsunami in the Mediterranean Sea 2000 B.C.-2000 A.D. *Advances in Natural and Technological Hazards Research*, Kluwer Academic Publisher: Dordrecht, 2000.

[9] Maramai, A., Graziani, L. & Tinti, S., Updating and revision of the European Tsunami Catalogue. *NATO Sciences Series: Submarine Landslides and Tsunami*, eds. A.C. Yalciner, E. Pelinovsky, E. Okal & C. Synolakis, Kluwer Academic Publishers: Dordrecht, pp. 25–32, 2003.

[10] Guidoboni, E. & Comastri, A., *Catalogue of Earthquakes and Tsunami in the Mediterranean Area from the 11th to the 15th Century.* Istituto Nazionale di Geofisica e Vulcanologia, Bologna, 2007.

[11] Tinti, S. & Maramai, A., Catalogue of tsunami generated in Italy and in Cote d'Azur, France: a step towards a unified catalogue of tsunami in Europe. *Annali di Geofisica*, **39**, pp. 1253–1299, 1996.

[12] Tinti, S., Maramai, A. & Graziani, L., The new catalogue of Italian tsunami. *Nature Hazards*, **33**, pp. 439–465, 2004.

[13] Tinti, S., Maramai, A. & Graziani, L., *The Italian Tsunami Catalogue (ITC)*. Version available on-line at http://www.ingv.it/servizi-erisorse/BD/catalogo-tsunami/catalogo-degli-tsunami-italiani, 2007.

[14] NGDC - National Geophysical Data Center. *Tsunami data at NGDC*. http://www.ngdc.noaa.gov/hazard/tsu_db.shtml, 2012.

[15] ICMMG - Institute of Computational Mathematics and Mathematical Geophysics. *On-line catalogs*. http://tsun.sscc.ru/On_line_Cat.htm, 2012.

[16] ITIC - International Tsunami Information Center, *Tsunami Database*. http://ioc3.unesco.org/itic/categories.php?category_no=72, 2012.

[17] United States Geological Survey National Earthquake Information Center. Web Site URL: http://earthquake.usgs.gov/earthquakes/recenteqsww/Quakes/us2009mdbi.php, 2012.

[18] Scheffers, A. & Kelletat, D., Sedimentologic and geomorphologic tsunami imprints worldwide—a review. *Earth-Science Reviews*, **63**, pp. 83–92, 2003.

[19] Dawson, A.G., Geomorphological effects of tsunami run-up and backwash. *Geomorphology*, **10**, pp. 83–94, 1994.

[20] Lorito, S., Tiberti, M.M., Basili, R., Piatanesi, A. & Valensise, G., Earthquake-generated tsunami in the Mediterranean Sea: scenarios of potential threats to Southern Italy. *Journal of Geophysical Research*, **113**, B01301, 2008.

[21] Tiberti, M.M., Lorito, S., Basili, R., Kastelic, V., Piatanesi, A. & Valensise, G., Scenarios of earthquake-generated tsunami for the Italian coast of the Adriatic Sea. *Pure and Applied Geophysics*, **165**, pp. 2117–2142, 2008.

[22] Lavigne, F., Paris, R., Wassmer, P., Gomez, C., Brunstein, D., Grancher, D., Vautier, F., Sartohadi, J., Setiawan, A., Syahnan, T.G., Fachrizal, B.W., Mardiatno, D., Widagdo,A., Cahyadi, R., Lespinasse, N. & Mahieu, L., Learning from a major disaster (Banda Aceh, December 26th, 2009): a methodology to calibrate simulation codes for tsunami inundation models. *Zeitschrift für Geomorphologie N.F.*, Suppl.-Bd. **146**, pp. 253–265, 2006.

[23] Dominey-Howes, D. & Papathoma, M., Validating a tsunami vulnerability assessment model (the PTVA Model) using field data from the 2004 Indian Ocean Tsunami. *Natural Hazard*, **40**, pp. 113–136, 2007.

[24] Imamura, F., Goto, K. & Ohkubo, S., A numerical model for the transport of a boulder by tsunami. *Journal Geophysical Research*, **113**, C01008, 2008. doi:10.1029/2007JC004170, 2008.

[25] Pignatelli, C., Sansò, P. & Mastronuzzi, G., Evaluation of tsunami flooding using geomorphologic evidence. *Marine Geology*, **260**, pp. 6–18, 2009.

[26] Mac Donald, L., *Curse of the Narrows: The Halifax Explosion of 1917*. HarperCollins: Toronto, 2005.

[27] Dawson, A.G., Long, D., Smith, D.E., Shi, S. & Foster, I.D.L., Tsunamis in the Norwegian Sea and North Sea caused by the Storegga submarine landslides. *Tsunamis in the World*, ed. S. Tinti, Kluwer Academic Publishers: The Netherlands, 1993.

[28] Bryant, E.A., Young, R.W. & Price, D.M., Tsunami as a major control on coastal evolution, Southeastern Australia. *Journal of Coastal Research*, **12**, pp. 831–840, 1996.

[29] Mastronuzzi, G. & Sansò, P., Boulder transport by catastrophic waves along the Ionian coast of Apulia (Southern Italy). *Marine Geology*, **170**, pp. 93–103, 2000.

[30] Mastronuzzi, G. & Sansò, P., The role of large earthquakes and tsunami in the Late Holocene evolution of Fortore River coastal plain (Apulia, Italy): a synthesis. *Geomorphology*, **138**, pp. 89–99, 2012.

[31] Gianfreda, F., Mastronuzzi, G. & Sansò, P., Impact of historical tsunamis on a sandy coastal barrier: an example from the northern Gargano coast, southern Italy. *Natural Hazard and Earth System Sciences*, **1(4)**, pp. 213–219, 2001.

[32] De Martini, P.M., Burrato, P., Pantosti, D., Maramai, A., Graziani, L. & Abramson, H., 2003. Identification of tsunami deposits and liquefaction features in the Gargano area (Italy): paleosismological implication. *Annals of Geophysics*, **46**, pp. 883–902, 2003.

[33] Vött, A., May, M., Brückner, H. & Brockmüller, S., Sedimentary evidence of late Holocene tsunami events near Lefkada Island (NW Greece). *Zeitschrift für Geomorphologie N.F.*, Suppl. Vol. 146, pp. 139–172, 2006.

[34] Vött, A., Brückner, H., May, M., Lang, F. & Brockmüller, S., Late Holocene tsunami imprint on *Actio headland at the entrance to the Ambrakian Gulf. Méditerranée*, **108**, pp. 43–57, 2007.

[35] Vött, A., Brückner, H., May, M., Lang, F., Herd, R. & Brockmüller, S., Strong tsunami impact on the Bay of Aghios Nikolaos and its environs (NW Greece) during Classical-Hellenistic times. *Quaternary International*, **181**, pp. 105–122, 2008a.

[36] Vött, A., Brückner, H., Brockmüller, S., Handl, M., May, S.M., Gaki-Papanastassiou, K., Herd, R., Lang, F., Maroukian, H., Nelle, O. & Papanastassiou, D., Traces of Holocene tsunami across the Sound of Lefkada, NW Greece. *Global and Planetary Change*, **66(1–2)**, pp. 112–128, 2008b.

[37] Vött, A., Brückner, H., May, S.M., Sakellariou, D., Nelle, O., Lang, F., Kapsimalis, V., Jahns, S., Herd, R., Handl, M. & Fountoulis, I., The Lake Voulkaria (Akarnania, NW Greece) palaeoenvironmental archive – a sediment trap for multiple tsunami impact since the mid-Holocene. *Zeitschrift für Geomorphologie N.F.*, Suppl. Issue 53, pp. 1–37, 2009b.

[38] Vött, A., Bareth, G., Brückner, H., Curdt, C., Fountoulis, I., Grapmayer, R., Hadler, H., Hoffmeister, D., Klasen, N., Lang, F., Masberg, P., May, S.M., Ntageretzis, K., Sakellariou, D. & Willershäuser, T., Beachrock-type calcarenitic tsunamites along the shores of the eastern Ionian Sea (western Greece) – case studies from Akarnania, the Ionian Islands and the western Peloponnese. *Zeitschrift für Geomorphologie*, **54**, Suppl. 3, pp. 1–50, 2010.

[39] Mastronuzzi, G., Pignatelli, C., Sansò, P. & Selleri, G., Boulder accumulations produced by the 20th February 1743 tsunami along the coast of southeastern Salento (Apulia region, Italy). *Marine Geology*, **242**, pp. 191–205, 2007.

[40] Regnauld, H., Nichol, S.L, Goff, J.R. & Fontugne, M., Maoris, middens and dune front accretion rate on the NE coast of New Zealand: resilience of a sedimentary system after a tsunami. *Géomorphologie*, **1**, pp. 45–54, 2004.

[41] Regnauld, H., Oszwald, J., Planchon, O., Pignatelli, C., Piscitelli, A., Mastronuzzi, G. & Audevard, A., Polygenic (tsunami and storm) deposits? A case study from Ushant Island, western France. *Zeitschrift für Geomorphologie*, **54**, Suppl. 3, pp. 197–217, 2010.

[42] Regnauld, H., Planchon, O. & Goff, J., Relative roles of structure, climate, and of a tsunami event on coastal evolution of the Falkland Archipelago. *Géomorphologie, reliefs, processus, environnement*, **1**, pp. 33–44, 2008.

[43] Bourgeois, J., Geologic effects and records of tsunami. *The Sea. Tsunami*, eds. A.R. Robinson, E.N. Bernard, Vol. 15. Harvard University Press: Cambridge, USA, pp. 55–91, 2009.

[44] Mastronuzzi, G. & Pignatelli, C., The boulder berms of Punta Saguerra (Taranto, Italy): a morphological imprint of 4th April, 1836 Rossano Calabro tsunami? *Earth Planets Space*, **64**, pp. 1–14, 2012.

[45] Shiki, T., Tachibana, T., Fujiwara, O., Goto, K., Nanayama, F. & Yamazaki, T., 2008. Characteristic Features of Tsunamiites. *Tsunamiites — Features and Implications*, eds. T. Shiki, Y. Tsuji, T. Yamasaki, K. Minoura, Elsevier: Amsterdam, pp. 319–340, 2008.

[46] Mastronuzzi, G., Brückner, H., Sansò, P. & Vött, A. (eds), Tsunami fingerprints in different archives – sediments, dynamics and modelling approaches. Zeitschrift für Geomorphologie, *N.F.*, vol. 54, Suppl. 3, 2010.

[47] Goto, K., Imamura, F., Koshimura, S., Mastronuzzi, G., Nishimura, Y. & Tanioka, Y. (eds), Tsunami: science, technology, and disaster mitigation. *Earth Planets and Space*, **64(10)**, pp. 785–990, 2012.

[48] Mastronuzzi, G. & Sansò, P., Large boulder accumulations by extreme waves along the Adriatic Coast of southern Apulia (Italy). *Quaternary International*, **120**, pp. 173–184, 2004.

[49] Scheffers, A. & Scheffers, S., Documentation of the impact of hurricane Ivan on the coastline of Bonaire (Netherlands Antilles). *Journal of Coastal Research*, **22(6)**, pp. 1437–1450, 2006.

[50] Barbano, M.S., Pirrotta, C. & Gerardi, F., Large boulders along the southeastern Ionian coast of Sicily: storm or tsunami deposits? *Marine Geology*, **275(14)**, pp. 140–154, 2010.

[51] Switzer, A.D. & Burston, J.M., Competing mechanisms for boulder deposition on the southeast Australian coast. *Geomorphology*, **114**, pp. 42–54, 2010.

[52] Switzer, A.D., Pucillo, K., Haredy, R.A., Jones, B.G. & Bryant, E.A., Sealevel, storms or tsunami; enigmatic sandsheet deposits in sheltered coastal embayment from southeastern New South Wales Australia. *Journal of Coastal Research*, **21**, pp. 655–663, 2005.

[53] Switzer, A.D. & Jones, B.G., Large-scale washover sedimentation in a freshwater lagoon from the southeast Australian coast: sea level change, tsunami or exceptionally large storm? *Holocene* **18**, pp. 787–803, 2008.

[54] Richmond, B.M., Watt, S., Buckley, M., Jaffe, B.E., Gelfenbaum, G. & Morton, R.A., Recent storm and tsunami coarse-clast deposit characteristics, southeast Hawaii. *Marine Geology*, **283(1–4)**, 2011.

[55] Paris, R., Fournier, J., Poizot, E., Etienne, S., Mortin, J., Lavigne, F. & Wassmer, P., Boulder and fine sediment transport and deposition by the 2004 tsunami in Lhok Nga (western Banda Aceh, Sumatra, Indonesia): a coupled offshore-onshore model. *Marine Geology*, **268**, pp. 43–54, 2010.

[56] Cita, M.B. & Aloisi, G., Deep-sea tsunami deposits triggered by the explosion of Santorini (3500 years BP), eastern Mediterranean. *Sedimentary Geology*, **135**, pp. 181–302, 2000.

[57] Gràcia, E., Vizcaino, A., Escutia, C., Asioli, A., Rodés, A., Pallàs, R., Garcia-Orellana, J., Lebreiro, S. & Goldfinger, C., Holocene earthquake record offshore Portugal (SW Iberia): testing turbidite paleoseismology in a slow-convergence margin. *Quaternary Science Reviews*, **29**, pp. 1156–1172, 2010.

[58] Lario, J., Luque, L., Zazo, C., Goy, J.L., Spencer, Ch., Cabero, A., Bardají, T., Borja, F., Dabrio, C.J., Civis, J., González-Delgado, J.Á., Borja, C. & Alonso-Azcárate, J., Tsunami vs. storm surge deposits: a review of the sedimentological and geomorphological records of extreme wave events (EWE) during the Holocene in the Gulf of Cádiz, Spain. *Zeitschrift für Geomorphologie*, **54**, Suppl. 3, pp. 301–316, 2010.

[59] Smedile, A., De Martini, P.M., Pantosti, D., Bellucci, L., Del Carlo, P., Gasperini, L., Pirrotta, C., Polonia, A. & Boschi, E., Possible tsunamis signatures from an integrated study in the Augusta Bay offshore (Eastern Sicily, Italy). *Marine Geology*, **281**, pp. 1–13, 2011.

[60] Smedile, A., De Martini, P.M. & Pantosti, D., Combining inland and offshore paleotsunami evidence: the Augusta Bay (eastern Sicily, ITALY) case study. *Natural Hazards and Earth System Sciences*, **12**, pp. 2557–2567, 2012.

[61] De Martini, P.M., Barbano, M.S., Smedile, A., Gerardi, F., Pantosti, D., Del Carlo, P. & Pirrotta, C., A unique 4000 year long geological record of multiple tsunami inundations in the Augusta Bay (eastern Sicily, Italy): paleoseismological implications. *Marine Geology*, **276**, pp. 42–57, 2010.

[62] Goodman-Tchernov, B.N., Dey, H.W., Reinhardt, E.G., McCoy, F. & Mart, Y., Tsunami waves generated by the Santorini eruption reached Eastern Mediterranean shores. *Geology*, **37**, pp. 943–946, 2009.

[63] Atwater, B.F., Evidence for great Holocene earthquakes along the outer coast of Washington State. *Science*, **236(4804)**, pp. 942–944, 1987.

[64] Bugge, T., Befring, S., Belderson, R.H., Eidvin, T., Jansen, E., Kenyon, N.H., Holtedahl, H. & Sejrup, H.P., A giant three-stage submarine slide off Norway. *Geo-Marine Letters* 7, pp. 191–198, 1987.

[65] Bugge, T., Belderson, R.H. & Kenyon, N.H., The Storegga Slide. *Philosophical Transactions of the Royal Society of London, Series A*, **325**, pp. 357–388, 1988.

[66] Grauert, M., Björck, S. & Bondevik, S., Storegga tsunami deposits in a coastal lake on SuDuroy, the Faroe Islands. *Boreas*, **30**, pp. 263–271. Oslo, 2001.

[67] Bondevik, S., Mangerud, J., Dawson, S., Dawson, A. & Lohne, Ø., Record-breaking height for 8000-year-old tsunami in the North Atlantic. *Eos*, **84(31)**, pp. 289–293, 2003.

[68] Engel, M., Brückner, H., Wennrich, V., Scheffers, A., Kelletat, D., Vött, A., Schäbitz, F., Daut, G., Willershäuser, T. & May, S.M., Coastal stratigraphies of eastern Bonaire (Netherlands Antilles): new insights into the palaeotsunami history of the southern Caribbean. *Sedimentary Geology*, **231**, pp. 14–30, 2010.

[69] Scheffers, A., Tsunami imprints on the Leeward Netherlands Antilles (Aruba, Curaçao, Bonaire) and their relation to other coastal problems. *Quaternary International*, **120**, pp. 163–172, 2004.

[70] Pignatelli, C., Scheffers, A., Scheffers, S. & Mastronuzzi, G., Evaluation of tsunami flooding from geomorphologic evidence in Bonaire (Netherlands Antilles). *Zeitschrift für Geomorphologie*, **54**, Suppl. 3, pp. 219–245, 2010a.

[71] Engel, M. & May, S.M., Bonaire's boulder fields revisited: evidence for Holocene tsunami impact on the Leeward Antilles. *Quaternary Science Reviews*, **54**, pp. 126–141, 2012.

[72] Vött, A., Brückner, H., Brockmüller, S., Handl, M., May, S.M., Gaki-Papanastassiou, K., Herd, R., Lang, F., Maroukian, H., Nelle, O. & Papanastassiou, D., Traces of Holocene tsunamis across the Sound of Lefkada, NW Greece. *Global and Planetary Change*, **66**, pp. 112–128, 2009c.

[73] May, S.M., Vött, A., Brückner, H. & Smedile, A. The Gyra washover fan in the Lefkada Lagoon, NW Greece – possible evidence of the 365 AD Crete earthquake and tsunami. *Earth Planets Space*, **64(10)**, 859–874, 2012.

[74] Shaw, B., Ambraseys, N.N., England, P.C., Floyd, M.A., Gorman, G.J., Higham, T.F.G., Jackson, J.A., Nocquet, J.-M., Pain, C.C. & Piggott, M.D., Eastern Mediterranean tectonics and tsunami hazard inferred from the AD 365 earthquake. *Nature Geoscience*, **1**, pp. 268–276, 2008.

[75] Vött, A., Brückner, H., May, M., Lang, F. & Brockmüller, S., Late Holocene tsunami imprint on Actio headland at the entrance to the Ambrakian Gulf. *Méditerranée*, **108**, pp. 43–57, 2007a.

[76] May, S.M., *Sedimentological, geomorphological and geochronological studies on Holocene tsunami in the Lefkada – Preveza area (NW Greece) and their implications for coastal evolution*, PhD thesis, Universität zu Köln, (http://kups.ub.uni-koeln.de/volltexte/2010/3189/), 2010.

[77] May, S.M., Vött, A., Brückner, H., Grapmayer, R., Handl, M. & Wennrich, V., The Lefkada barrier and beachrock system (NW Greece) – controls on coastal evolution and the significance of extreme wave events. *Geomorphology*, **139–140**, pp. 330–347, 2012.

[78] Goff, J.R., McFadgen, B.G. & Chagué-Goff, C., Sedimentary differences between the 2002 Easter storm and the 15th-century Okoropunga tsunami, southeastern North Island, New Zealand. *Marine Geology*, **204**, pp. 235–250, 2004.

[79] Goff, J. & Chagué-Goff, C., Cetaceans and tsunamis – whatever remains, however improbable, must be the truth? *Natural Hazards and Earth System Sciences*, **9**, pp. 855–857, 2009.

[80] Bujalesky, G.G., Tsunami overtopping fan and erosive scarps at Atlantic Coast of Tierra del Fuego. *Journal of Coastal Research*, **28(2)**. pp. 442–456, 2012.

[81] Sugawara, D., Minoura, K., Imamura, F., Takahashi, T. & Shuto, N., A huge sand dome formed by the 1854 earthquake tsunami in Suruga Bay, Central Japan. *ISET Journal of Earthquake Technology*, **42(4)**, pp. 147–158, 2005.

[82] Nichol, S.L., Lian, O.B. & Carter, C.H., Sheet-gravel evidence for a late Holocene tsunami run-up on beach dunes, Great Barrier Island, New Zealand. *Sedimentary Geology*, **155**, pp. 129–145, 2003.

[83] Szczuciński, W., Kokociński, M., Rzeszewski, M., Chagué-Goff, C., Cachão, M., Goto, K. & Sugawara, D., Sediment sources and sedimentation processes of 2011 Tohoku-oki tsunami deposits on the Sendai Plain, Japan — insights from diatoms, nannoliths and grain size distribution. *Sedimentary Geology*, 2012, http://dx.doi.org/10.1016/j.sedgeo.2012.07.019.

[84] Szczucinski, W., Niedzielski, P., Rachlewicz, G., Sobczyski, T., Ziola, A., Kowalski, A., Lorenc, S. & Siepak, J., Contamination of tsunami sediments in a coastal zone inundated by the 26 December 2004 tsunami in Thailand. *Environmental Geology*, **49(2)**, pp. 321–331, 2005.

[85] Richmond, B., Szczuciński, W., Chagué-Goff, C., Goto, K., Sugawara, D., Witter, R., Tappin, D.R., Jaffe, B., Fujino, S., Nishimura, Y. & Goff, J., 2012. Erosion, deposition and landscape change on the Sendai coastal plain, Japan, resulting from the March 11, 2011 Tohoku-oki tsunami. *Sedimentary Geology*. 2012, http://dx.doi.org/10.1016/j.sedgeo.2012.08.005.

[86] Kawana, T. & Pirazzoli, P., Re-examination of the Holocene emerged shore-lines in Orabu and Shimoji Islands, the South Ryukyus, Japan. *Quaternary Research*, **28**, pp. 419–426, 1990.

[87] Nishimura, Y. & Miyaji, N., Tsunami deposits from the 1993 Southwest Hokkaido earthquake and the 1640 Hokkaido Komagatake eruption, northern Japan. Tsunami: 1992–1994, their Generation, Dynamics, and Hazard, eds. K. Satake, F. Imamura. *Pure and Applied Geophysics*, **144 (3–4)**, pp. 719–733, 1995.

[88] Goto, K., Miyagi, K., Kawamata, H. & Imamura, F., Discrimination of boulders deposited by tsunami and storm waves at Ishigaki Island, Japan. *Marine Geology*, **269**, pp. 34–45, 2010b.

[89] Goto, K., Chavanich, S.A., Imamura, F., Kunthasap, P., Matsui, T., Minoura, K., Sugawara, D. & Yanagisawa, H., Distribution, origin and transport process of boulders deposited by the 2004 Indian Ocean tsunami at Pakarang Cape, Thailand. *Sedimentary Geology*, **202**, pp. 821–837, 2007.

[90] Jones, B. & Hunter, I.G., Very large boulders on the coast of Grand Cayman, the effects of giant waves on rocky shorelines. *Journal of Coastal Research*, **8**, pp. 763–774, 1992.

[91] Bryant, E.A. & Young, R.W., Bedrock-sculpturing by tsunami, south coast New South Wales, Australia. *Journal of Geology*, **104**, pp. 565–582, 1996.

[92] Young, R.W., Bryant, E.A. & Price, D.M., Catastrophic wave (tsunami?) transport of boulders in southern New South Wales, Australia. *Zeitschrift für Geomorphologie N.F.*, **40(2)**, pp. 191–207, 1996.

[93] Hearty, J.P., Boulder deposits from large waves during the last interglaciation on North Eleuthera Island, Bahamas. *Quaternary Research*, **48**, pp. 326–338, 1997.

[94] Whelan, F. & Kelletat D. 2005: Boulder deposits on the southern Spanish Atlantic coast: possible evidence for the 1755 AD Lisbon tsunami? *Science of Tsunami Hazards*, **23(3)**, pp. 25–38, 2005.

[95] Scicchitano, G., Monaco, C. & Tortorici, L., Large boulder deposits by tsunami waves along the Ionian coast of south-eastern Sicily (Italy). *Marine Geology*, **238(1–4)**, pp. 75–91, 2007.

[96] Kelletat, D. & Schellmann, G., Tsunamis on Cyprus. Field evidences and 14C dating results. *Zeitschrift für Geomorphologie N.F.*, **46**, pp. 19–34, 2002.

[97] Scheffers, A., Kelletat, D., Vött, A., May, S.M. & Scheffers, S., Late Holocene tsunami traces on the western and southern coastlines of the Peloponnesus (Greece). *Earth Planetary Science Letters*, **269**, pp. 271–279, 2008.

[98] Goff, J., Dudley, W.C., deMaintenon, M.J., Cain, G. & Coney, J.P., The largest local tsunami in 20th century Hawaii. *Marine Geology*, **226**, pp. 65–79, 2006.

[99] Kennedy, D.M., Tannock, K.L., Crozier, M.J. & Rieser, U., Boulders of MIS 5 age deposited by a tsunami on the coast of Otago, New Zealand. *Sedimentary Geology*, **200**, pp. 222–231, 2007.

[100] Frohlich, C., Hornbach, M.J., Taylor, F.W., Shen, C.C., Moala, A., Morton, A.E. & Kruger, J., Huge erratic boulders in Tonga deposited by a prehistoric tsunami. *Geology*, **37(2)**, pp. 131–134, 2009.

[101] Williams, D.M. & Hall, A.M., Cliff-top megaclast deposits of Ireland, a record of extreme waves in the North Atlantic—storms or tsunami? *Marine Geology*, **206**, pp. 101–117, 2004.

[102] Hall, A.M., Hansom, J.D., Williams, D.M. & Jarvis, P., Distribution, geomorphology and lithofacies of cliff top storm deposits: examples from the high-energy coasts of Scotland and Ireland. *Marine Geology*, **232**, pp. 131–155, 2006.

[103] Hansom, J.D., Barltrop, N.D.P. & Hall, A.M., Modelling the processes of cliff-top erosion and deposition under extreme storm waves. *Marine Geology*, **253**, pp. 36–50, 2008.

[104] Mastronuzzi, G., Pignatelli, C. & Sansò, P., Boulder fields: a valuable morphological indicator of paleotsunami in the Mediterranean Sea. *Zeitschrift für Geomorphologie, N.F.*, Suppl.-Bd. **146**, pp. 173–194, 2006.

[105] Bourrouilh-Le Jan, F.G., Beck, C. & Gorsline, D.S., Catastrophic events (hurricanes,next term tsunami and others) and their sedimentary records: Introductory notes and new concepts for shallow water deposits. *Sedimentary Geology*, **199(1–2)**, pp. 1–11, 2007.

[106] Scheffers, A., Paleotsunami in the Caribbean. Field evidences and datings from Aruba, Curaçao and Bonaire. *Essener Geographique Arbeiten*, **33**, 2002a.

[107] Scheffers, A., Paleotsunami evidences of tsunami from boulder deposits on Aruba, Curaçao and Bonaire. *Science of Tsunami Hazard*, **20(1)**, pp. 26–37, 2002b.

[108] McFadgen, B.G. & Goff, J.R., 2007. Tsunami in the archaeological record of New Zealand. *Sedimentary Geology*, **200**, pp. 263–274, 2007.

[109] Goff, J., Weiss, R., Courtney C. & Dominey-Howes D., Testing the hypothesis for tsunami boulder deposition from suspension. *Marine Geology*, **277(1–4)**, pp. 73–77, 2010.

[110] Spiske, M., Böröcz, Z. & Bahlburg, H., The role of porosity in discriminating between tsunami and hurricane emplacement of boulders – a case study from the Lesser Antilles, southern Caribbean. *Earth and Planetary Science Letters*, **268**, pp. 384–396, 2008.

[111] Benner, R., Browne, T., Brückner, H., Kelletat, D. & Scheffers, A., Boulder transport by waves: progress in physical modelling. *Zeitschrift für Geomorphologie*, **54**, Suppl. 3, pp. 127–146, 2010.

[112] Kawana, T. & Nakata, K., The Meiwa tsunami and the submarine crustal movement. *Journal of the Society of Historical Studies*, **3**, pp. 181–194, 1987.

[113] Goto, K., Okada, K. & Imamura, F., Importance of the initial waveform and coastal profile for the tsunami transport of boulders. *Polish Journal of Environmental Studies*, **18**, pp. 53–61, 2009a.

[114] Goto, K., Okada, K. & Imamura, F., Characteristics and hydrodynamics of boulders transported by storm wave at Kudaka Island, Japan. *Marine Geology*, **262**, pp. 14–24, 2009b.

[115] Goto, K., Kawana, T. & Imamura, F., Historical and geological evidence of boulders deposited by tsunami, southern Ryukyu Island, Japan. *Earth-Science Reviews*, **102**, 77–99, 2010a.

[116] Mastronuzzi, G., Tsunami in Mediterranean Sea. *The Egyptian Journal of Environmental Change*, **2(1)**, pp. 1–9, 2010.

[117] Gianfreda, F., Miglietta, M. & Sansò, P., Tornadoes in Southern Apulia (Italy). *Natural Hazards*, **34**, pp. 71–89, 2005.

[118] Emanuel, K.A., Increasing destructiveness of tropical cyclones over the past 30 years. *Nature*, **436**, pp. 686–688, 2005.

[119] Fita, L., Romero, R., Luque, A., Emanuel, K. & Ramis, C., Analysis of the environments of seven Mediterranean tropical-like storms using an axisymmetric, nonhydrostatic, cloud resolving model. *Natural Hazard Earth Systems Science*, **7**, pp. 41–56, 2007.

[120] Dominey-Howes, D.T.M., Documentary and geological records of tsunami in the Aegean Sea region of Greece and their potential value to risk assessment and disaster management. *Natural Hazards*, **25**, pp. 195–224, 2002.

[121] Mastronuzzi, G. & Sansò, S., Coastal geomorphology and tsunami vulnerability. The case study of Apulia region (Italy). *Geografia Fisica e Dinamica Quaternaria*, **29(2)**, pp. 83–91, 2006.

[122] Weiss, R., Wünnemann, K. & Bahlburg, H., Numerical modelling of generation, propagation and run-up of tsunami caused by oceanic impacts: model strategy and technical solutions. *Geophysical Journal International*, **167(1)**, pp. 77–88, 2006.

[123] Jaffe, B.E. & Gelfenbaum, G., 2007. A simple model for calculating tsunami flow speed from tsunami deposits. *Sedimentary Geology*, **200**, pp. 347–361, 2007.

[124] Jaffe, B., Buckley, M., Richmond, B., Strotz, L., Etienne, S., Clark, K., Watt, S., Gelfenbaum, G. & Goff, J., 2011. Flow speed estimated by inverse modeling of sandy sediment deposited by the 29 September 2009 tsunami near Satitoa, east Upolu, Samoa. *Earth-Science Reviews*, **107**, pp. 23–37, 2011.

[125] Jaffe, B.E., Goto, K., Sugawara, D., Richmond, B.M., Fujino, S. & Nishimura, Y., Flow speed estimated by inverse modeling of the sandy tsunami deposit: results from 11 March 2011 tsunami on the coastal plain near the Sendai Airport, Honshu, Japan. *Sedimentary Geology*, **282**, pp. 90–109, 2012.

[126] Nott J., Extremely high-energy wave deposits inside Great Barrier Reef, Australia: determining the cause – tsunami or tropical cyclone. *Marine Geology*, **141**, pp. 193–207, 1997.

[127] Nott J., Waves, coastal boulder deposits and the importance of the pre-transport setting. *Earth and Planetary Science Letters*, **210**, pp. 269–276, 2003.

[128] Noormets, R., Crook, K.A.W. & Felton, E.A., Sedimentology of rocky shorelines: 3. Hydrodynamics of megaclast emplacement and transport on a shore platform, Oahu, Hawaii. *Sedimentary Geology*, **172**, pp. 41–65, 2004.

[129] Noormets, R., Felton, E.A. & Crook, K.A.W., Sedimentology of rocky shorelines: 2. Shoreline megaclasts on the north shore of Oahu, Hawaii – origins and history. *Sedimentary Geology*,W **150**, pp. 31–45, 2002.

[130] Pignatelli, C., Ferilli, S., Capolongo, D., Marsico, A., Milella, M., Pennetta, L., Piscitelli, A. & Mastronuzzi, G., Evidenze morfologiche, rilievo digitale ed applicazioni informatiche al fine della valutazione del limite di inondazione da tsunami. *Italian Journal of Remote Sensing*, **42(2)**, pp. 129–142, 2010b.

[131] Nandasena, N.A.K., Paris, R. & Tanaka, N., Reassessment of hydrodynamic equations: minimum flow velocity to initiate boulder transport by high energy events (storms, tsunamis). *Marine Geology*, **281**, pp. 70–84, 2011.

[132] Marsico, A., Pignatelli, C., Piscitelli, A., Mastronuzzi, G. & Pennetta, L., *Ricostruzione digitale di blocchi accumulati da eventi estremi in Italia meridionale*. Atti 13 Conferenza Nazionale ASITA, 1–4 dicembre 2009, pp. 1377–1385, 2009.

[133] Mastronuzzi, G. & Pignatelli, C., Determination of tsunami inundation model using terrestrial laser scanner techniques. *The Tsunami Threat, Research and Technologies*, ed N.-A. Mörner, INTECH: Croatia, pp. 219–236, 2011.

[134] Hoffmeister, D., Ntageretzis, K., Aasen, H., Curdt, C., Hadler, H., Willershäuser, T., Bareth, G., Brückner, H. & Vött, A., 3D model-based estimations of volume and mass of high-energy dislocated boulders in coastal areas of Greece by terrestrial laser scanning. *Zeitschrift für Geomorphologie, N.F.*, Supplementary Issue (accepted), 2012.

[135] Imamura, F., Yoshida, I. & Moore, A., 2001. Numerical study of the 1771 Meiwa tsunami at Ishigaki Island, Okinawa and the movement of the tsunami stones. *Annual Journal of Coastal Engineering*, JSCE, **48**, pp. 346–350, 2001.

[136] Hills, J.G. & Mader, C.L., Tsunami produced by the impacts of the small asteroids. *Annals of the New York Academy of Sciences*, **822**, pp. 381–394, 1997.

CHAPTER 2

An inverse algorithm for reconstructing an initial Tsunami waveform

Tatyana Voronina
Institute of Computational Mathematics and Mathematical Geophysics SB, RAS, Russia.

Abstract

This chapter proposes a new approach to reconstructing the initial tsunami waveform in a tsunami source area, which is based on the inversion of remote measurements of water-level data. The inverse problem in question is treated as an ill-posed problem of the hydrodynamic inversion with tsunami tide gauge records; hence, it imposes some restrictions on the use of mathematical techniques. Tsunami wave propagation is considered within the scope of the linear shallow-water theory. Numerical simulation is based on the finite difference algorithm and the method of splitting. The ill-posed inverse problem of reconstructing initial tsunami waveforms is regularized by means of a least square inversion using the truncated singular value decomposition approach. This method allows one to control instability of the numerical solution and to win through to obtain an acceptable result in spite of the ill-posedness of the problem. Such an approach provides a more accurate insight into potentialities intrinsic of the sea level network – used as a database for reconstructing a tsunami source. The sea level data inversion due to the methodology suggested could be used to obtain appropriate assumptions about the static deformation in the source area, as initial condition for the tsunami generation and for the widespread numerical modeling of real historical tsunamis, to verify algorithms and codes in the tsunami research. The approach proposed could be particularly effective as one of the supplementary tools for the early warning against frequent and destructive near-field tsunamis.

1 Introduction

People are surrounded by a variety of natural systems, the main part of them being guideless. Earthquakes and tsunamis just belong to such events. They bring disasters that cannot be completely prevented, but it is possible to mitigate them due to the timely prediction. What is a tsunami? It is now more important than ever to understand the nature and characteristics of tsunamis and their potential hazards to coastal communities.

The beginning of the new millennium was marked with a formidable challenge to humanity from the World Ocean. Thousands of miles from the scene could be seen in real time how the ruthless dark waters quickly and inexorably devour anything that until recently has been homes, gardens, fields – human life as is. Thus, on March 11, 2011, humanity saw terrible tsunami images of the coast of Japan. This day, a massive earthquake (9.3 Mw) has hit the northeast Japan, triggering a tsunami that has caused extensive damage. The giant waves deluged cities and rural areas, sweeping away cars, homes, buildings, a train, boats, leaving a path of death and devastation in its wake. More than 20,000 people were killed when the earthquake and tsunami struck. The tsunami in Japan recalled the 2004 disaster in the Indian Ocean. The Andaman tsunami that occurred on 26 December 2004 has caused severe damage to properties and the loss of 300,000 lives on the affected coastal regions – the deadliest tsunami in the world history. These mega-events served as a wake-up call to the coastal communities of many countries to stand up to the adverse impacts of future tsunamis. The first national tsunami warning system was organized in the late 1940s in the United States after the tsunami that occurred on Alaska Aleutian Islands, in 1946, and originally confined to the Pacific region; the system has been expanded to the Caribbean and the North Atlantic. The international Tsunami Warning Systems (TWS), involving 26 countries, was established after the Chilean tsunami in 1960, which generated a Pacific-wide tsunami causing extensive damage in various countries. Although not so frequent, destructive tsunamis have also generated in the Atlantic and the Indian Oceans, the Mediterranean Sea, and even within smaller bodies of water, like the Sea of Marmara, in Turkey. An early warning system for the Indian Ocean began operating in 2006. The absence of the tsunami warning system in the Indian Ocean in 2004 caused immense victims and highlighted the urgent need for robust international early warning systems. Today, a global international tsunami warning system acts under the auspices of the United Nations.

First of all, the mitigation of tsunami disasters demands modernization of the existing TWS which, in turn, requires scientific, engineering, and sociological research in order to assess probabilistic tsunami hazard coastal regions at risk and ultimately to produce appropriate inundation maps. All include an advanced technology of recordings of data of seismic, sea level, and pressure changes caused by tsunamis, on-line data processing with a greater accuracy.

It should be noted that tsunami warnings are extremely complicated, the statistics of issued warnings being far from satisfactory. For the last 55 years, up to 75% of warnings for regional tsunamis have turned out to be false, while each TWS has had at least a few cases of missing dangerous tsunamis, because seismic data often are translated to tsunami data not exactly. As a tsunami may be less than 1 m high on the surface of the open ocean, it is difficult to be noticed by sailors. The increasing reliability of the tsunami warnings can be achieved in part by numerical modeling, which allows estimating an expected propagation and run up, wave heights, inundation distances, current velocities, and arrival times of tsunami at the protected coastal communities.

The intensive development of numerical simulation of real tsunamis began in the late sixties of the twientieth century. Primarily, much attention was given to these problems in the Ring of Fire countries (USA, Japan, Canada, Australia, and Malaysia) and in Europe. Advanced computer technologies have given an impetus to the development of numerical modeling of tsunamis. The first studies in this area were carried out by Abe [1], Aida [2], Satake [5, 6] in Japan, by Mader [3], Bernard [4], Gonzalez et al. [7], Titov et al. [8, 9] in the United States, Tinti et al. [10] in Europe. They and other scientists have influenced on forming the TWS in all the countries.

In Russia, the study of the tsunami phenomenon started after the Kamchatka tsunami in 1952. Academician Soloviev [11] has pioneered some of the aspects of understanding and predicting tsunamis. Following his ideas several groups of scientists and specialists (in Moscow, Nizhny Novgorod, Leningrad, Novosibirsk, etc.) have studied at different times various aspects of this major problem. In the seventies of the previous century, numerous studies on the tsunami waves were carried out in scientific institutions of the Siberian Branch of the Russian Academy of Sciences to address the problems of numerical modeling of tsunami waves. Robust new computational algorithms and software were created by Gusiakov and Chubarov [12], Chubarov et al. [13, 14], Marchuk et al. [15], Hakimzyanov and Fedotova [16], etc. Commissioned by UNESCO the group headed by Shokin Y.Iv created the maps of the tsunami travel times (TTT) in the Pacific [17]. Their investigations correspond to the adopted concept of development of the National Tsunami Warning System of the Russian Federation. Their research has made possible evaluating tsunami risk through numerical simulation, in particular, estimating wave heights and run up for mitigation and warning. The specialized data-processing system WinITDB ITRIS (2007) and HTDB/WLD (2012), Historical Tsunami Database for the World Ocean (2012) (Web-version is available at http://tsun.sscc.ru/nh/tsunami.php) were pioneered by Gusiakov [18]. These information systems are developed by a tsunami research team for the purpose of the hydrodynamic modeling of tsunamis using computer models.

In case of a near field tsunami that are generated by sources located at short distances of less than 300 km and that are the most devastating, the disaster management has a little time for decision making. Mathematical modeling of tsunamis is to provide tsunami-resilient communities with reliable information of inundation heights and arrival times for the purpose to immediate protective measures. There are two important aspects of the assessment of tsunami risk in the coastal areas: the initial waves generated at the source area and provided further distractive strength of tsunami impact and the subsequent propagation. Generally accepted numerical tsunami models are based on the long-wave theory, valid for a small amplitude and nondispersive propagation within linear and nonlinear shallow water models and recorded either in the Cartesian or in the spherical coordinate system. There are many of actively used codes that are based on this theory.

One of the first among software was developed as a part of the IUGG / IOC Time Project with support from UNESCO program TUNAMI (Tohoku University's Numerical-Analysis Model for Investigation of Tsunami) and its modifications TUNAMI-N2 by Goto et al. [19]. This code was updated by many authors, one of successful modifications was made by Kurkin *et al.* [20] in the Institute of Applied Physics in Russia.

The first version of the MOST model (method of splitting tsunami) was developed by Titov and Gonzalez [21]. Numerical simulation was based on the finite difference algorithm for the nonlinear equations and the method of splitting. Generation of the initial perturbation uses a script based on seismic models [21]. This MOST model takes into account the Earth's curvature to predict tsunami travel over a long open ocean distance. It also accurately predicts the water-surface elevation and wave heights. Generation of the initial perturbation uses a script based on seismic models Okada [22].

The software system NEREUS was created by Chubarov *et al.* [23] in the Institute of Computational Technologies SB RAS and based on a modified difference scheme of MacCormack for shallow water equations in a conservative form. This code could provide numerical modeling of propagation and calculating run up heights. Computational experiments are conducted for a representative set of model sources of different power and distance for the Far Eastern coast of Russia.

Usage of more complicated models allows retracing more details of the wave behavior for example, a weakly nonlinear model by Nwogu [24], a fully nonlinear potential flow theory that was used to reproduce details of breaking wavefronts Lynett and Liu [25] or Pelinovsky [26] the long-wave nonlinear-dispersion model of the tsunami.

The software code FUNWAVE was based on the nonlinear dispersive equations obtained [27], originally destined for the wave modeling in the coastal zone. However, further development of this approach makes possible to apply it to various cases of wave propagations and run up simulation. The integrated software code GEOWAVE [28] includes both the Tsunami Open and Progressive Initial Conditions System (TOPICS) and the fully nonlinear Boussinesq water wave model FUNWAVE. TOPICS [29] is used to obtain the initial condition for several parametric scenarios of tsunami generation: underwater slides, underwater slumps, debris flows, and pyroclastic flows. The tsunami source predicted by TOPICS is introduced as an initial condition into FUNWAVE.

An attempt to make a comparative estimate of the efficiency of the known computational models and programming systems of the hydrodynamic tsunami simulation based on these models was undertaken in Shokin *et al.* [30]. According to the results obtained, all the above-mentioned models are almost identical to the computational accuracy of the algorithms and to the hydrodynamic accuracy of mathematical models. This fact allows one to state that the effects of nonlinear dispersion terms are of minor importance of the overall wave behavior of concern, such as amplitudes and run up heights.

Apparently, the most effective approach to solving the problem of numerical tsunami simulation is to use various models at different stages of the tsunami wave existence.

This review of the currently known tsunami simulation software codes is far from being exhaustive and is intended to show the diversity of approaches. The list of commonly used hydrodynamic approaches and the modeling codes descriptions for the problem of generation and propagation of the tsunami waves can be found, for example, in Levin and Nosov [31] and *Gusiakov et al.* [32].

Recently, the devastating tsunamis have acutely put forward the problem for their timely warning and, as consequence, the importance of the accurate tsunami simulation. It can be expected that the development of numerical modeling of tsunami waves will increase the reliability of tsunami forecasting. An important part of tsunami simulation is to gain some insight into a tsunami source. An earthquake occurred near the seabed may produce a co-seismic deformation that can cause a displacement in the sea floor that can in turn cause an initial sea surface deformation that result in a tsunami wave. This sea surface deformation will be called an initial tsunami waveform or simply a tsunami source. It is well known that only some time after an event, by analyzing various seismic, tidal, and other data, it becomes possible to estimate the tsunami source basic characteristics. Slow and often inaccurate estimation of the earthquake source parameters remains an obstacle to on-time tsunami predictions. Thus, a demand arose for a more effective method in the near-field, where a warning should be issued in 5–10 min. Numerical modeling of a tsunami source is an important tool of assessment and mitigation of the negative effects of tsunamis. The sea level data inversion could be used to obtain appropriate assumptions about the static deformation in the source area as initial condition for the tsunami simulation.

There are many approaches to creating the method based on the inversion of near-field water-level data.

Satake [5, 6] was the first to propose a tsunami waveform inversion method using Green's function technique to invert a co-seismic slip from observed tide gauges data. *A priori* information about the tsunami source played an essential role in his inversion method. It is quite a common practice to determine the slip distribution along the fault of tsunamigenic earthquakes on the basis of tsunami data, eventually using the joint inversion of tsunami and geodetic data. A similar approach was used by Johnson *et al.* [33, 34]. In the method proposed by Tinti *et al.* [10] and Piatanesi *et al.* [35], the inversion of tide-gauge records for the initial waveform determination was carried out by the least-squares inversion of a rectangular system of linear equations. One of the main advantages of this method is that it does not require *a priori* assumption of a fault plane solution: actually, this method is completely independent of any particular source model, but its serious limitation is using only the linear propagation models. An adjoint method for tsunami waveform inversion was proposed by Pires and Miranda [36] as an alternative to the technique based on Green's functions of the linear long wave model [5]. The tsunami's initial condition was searched by way of the optimization of the sets of unknown parameters of a linear or a nonlinear function defined as an initial state. This method has the advantage of being able to use the nonlinear shallow water equations, or other appropriate equation sets. A large number of papers is devoted to estimating the slip distribution of an earthquake in the tsunami center by the inversion of teleseismic body waves (Baba *et. al* [37]).

This chapter is concerned with a new approach to solving the problem of reconstructing a tsunami source. It is well known that the inverse problem at hand is ill-posed, which imposes some restrictions on the use of mathematical techniques. To this end, we have developed a technique based on the least-squares inversion using the truncated singular value decompositio (SVD) approach. The inverse problem to infer the initial sea displacement is considered as a usual ill-posed problem of the hydrodynamic inversion of tsunami tide-gauge records. Mathematically, the forward problem, that is, the calculation of synthetic tide-gage records from the initial water elevation field, is based on a linear shallow-water system of differential equations in the rectangular coordinates. This system is approximated by the explicit–implicit finite difference scheme on a uniform rectangular grid; hence, a system of linear algebraic equations will be obtained. The ill-posed inverse problem is regularized by means of least-squares inversion using the truncated *SVD* approach. In this method, the inverse operator is replaced by its restriction to a subspace spanned by a finite number of the first right singular vectors [38]. The so-called *r*-solution [39] is produced by a numerical process. The quality of the solution is defined by relative errors of the tsunami source reconstruction.

On both practical and theoretical grounds it is of interest to answer the following questions: (1) What minimum number of the sea level records (marigrams) should be used to recover a tsunami source well enough? (2) How accurately a tsunami source can be reconstructed, based on recordings at a given tide gouge network? (3) Is it possible to improve the quality of reconstructing a tsunami source by distinguishing the most informative part of the initial observation system? For answering these questions within the framework of approach proposed, we have carried out a series of numerical experiments with synthetic data and a real bathymetry.

Based on the characteristics of a given tide gauges network, the proposed method allows one to control the numerical instability of the resultant solutions and hence to obtain an acceptable result in spite of the ill-posedness of the problem. The first few experiments have shown that this approach is effective in tsunami source reconstruction [38].

Thus, the results obtained strongly depend on the signal-to-noise ratio due to the ill-posedness of the problem. Since the tsunami wave is a low-frequency phenomenon as compared to the background noise, an appropriate filtering of the calculated signals was made. The numerical results have been found to be highly sensitive to the spatial distribution of the monitoring stations as related to the local bathymetric features. It was found, as in other methods, that the inversion skill of tsunami sources increases with the improvement of azimuthal and temporal coverage of assimilated tide gauges stations.

2 Statement of the problem

It is a normal practice to assume that a tsunami process onset is an abrupt displacement of huge volumes of water induced by the seafloor displacement when the seafloor is suddenly raised or lowered, or be caused by a violent horizontal displacement of water, as may occur in the case of a submarine landslide. Usually these sea floor movements may be triggered by seismic activities. An initial sea surface deformation is presumed to be equal to the co-seismic vertical displacement of the sea floor. In view of the fact that most tsunamis that caused damage were generated by sources, located at short distances of less than 300 km, the curvature of the Earth is neglected in this research. This approach is widely applied to the numerical modeling of the tsunami generation.

Mathematically, the problem of reconstructing the original tsunami waveform in the source area is formulated as determination of spatial distribution of an oscillation source using remote measurements on a finite set of points, later called as "receivers." One of the most difficult and poorly understood aspects of the tsunami waves propagation is their interaction with the coastline. In this chapter, we have chosen the simplest of approximate models – with a condition of total reflection from the solid wall, consisting in nullifying the normal derivative of the function describing the free-surface elevation with respect to the external normal vector. Consider an xyz-coordinate system and direct the z-axis downwards. The plane $\{z = 0\}$ corresponds to the undisturbed water surface. Consider the aquatic part Φ of a rectangular domain $\Pi = \{(x;y) : 0 \le x \le X; 0 \le y \le Y\}$ on the plane $\{z = 0\}$ with piecewise-linear boundaries on dry land Γ and straight-line sea boundaries. Let $\Omega = \{(x,y) : x_0 \le x \le x_M; y_0 \le y \le y_N)\}$ be a tsunami source subdomain of Φ. A tsunami is a series of waves traveling at high speeds, for long periods and with long wavelengths, generated by an abrupt displacement of large volumes of water in the ocean. The process of the tsunami wave initialization could be simulated within the scope of the shallow water theory, when water elevation $\eta(x,y,t)$ over the undisturbed state satisfies the following scalar wave equation:

$$\eta_{tt} = \operatorname{div}(gh(x,y)\operatorname{grad}\eta) + f_{tt}(x,y,t) \tag{1}$$

with initial condition:

$$\eta|_{t=0} = 0; \quad \eta_{t|t=0} = 0; \tag{2}$$

On the coastline, the total reflection condition is used, on the sea boundaries $\Gamma_1 : y = 0, \Gamma_2 : y = Y, \Gamma_3 : x = X$, absorbing boundary conditions are used (see [47]):

$$c_{\Gamma_1}\eta_{yt} + \eta_{tt} + \frac{c_{\Gamma_1}^2}{2}\eta_{xx}|_{y=0} = 0;$$

$$\frac{\partial\eta}{\partial n}|_{\Gamma} = 0, -c_{\Gamma_2}\eta_{yt} + \eta_{tt} + \frac{c_{\Gamma_2}^2}{2}\eta_{xx}|_{y=Y} = 0; \tag{3}$$

$$-c_{\Gamma_3}\eta_{xt} + \eta_{tt} + \frac{c_{\Gamma_3}^2}{2}\eta_{yy}|_{x=X} = 0;$$

where c_{Γ_i} is the velocity on the appropriate boundary.

Water level oscillations $\eta_0(x,y,t), 0 \le t \le T$ are known on a line γ (a smooth curve without self-intersection)

$$\eta_0(x,y;t)|_{\gamma} = \eta_0(x(s),y(s);t);(x(s),y(s)) \in \gamma, 0 \le s \le S, \quad 0 \le t \le T. \tag{4}$$

In (1), $h(x,y)$ is the depth of the ocean, g is the acceleration of gravity, and function $f(x, y, t)$ describes sea floor motion in the tsunami source area. The tsunami propagation velocity is defined as $c(x,y)=\sqrt{gh(x,y)}$. The above problem has a unique solution only if the source function allows factorization [40], that is, the time and spatial variables can be separated: $f(x,y,t)=H(t)\cdot\varphi(x,y)$, where $H(t)$ is the Heaviside step function. The function $\varphi(x,y)$ describes the initial sea surface deformation, which is a co-seismic vertical displacement of the sea floor. In addition, $\varphi(x,y)$ is supposed to belong to the class $C_c(\Omega)\cap\eta_2^1(\Omega)$.

3 Inverse method

Denote by A the operator of solution of the forward problem, which is defined by the following way: for each given $\varphi(x,y)$ solve the Cauchy problem (1)–(3) and restrict its solution to the line γ:

$$\mathcal{A}\varphi(x,y)=\xi(s,t). \tag{5}$$

We assume that function $h(x,y)$ is continuously differentiable (this assumption does not necessarily hold in the experiments). Then, as shown by Ladyzhenskaya [41, Ch. IV], a solution of the initial-boundary value problem (1)–(3) exists and belongs to an energy class of solutions. Consequently, the trace of this solution is defined for each $t\in(0,T)$ on the curve γ as an element of $W_2^{1/2}(\gamma(s),0\leq s\leq S)$ for sufficiently large S. In turn, as shown in [42] $W_2^{1/2}(\gamma(s),0\leq s\leq S)$ is compactly embedded in the space $L_2(\gamma(s))$. Thus, function $\xi(s,t)$ for each fixed t is an element of the space $L_2(0,L)$, and its norm continuously depends on t in this space. We can consider the operator A: $W_2^1(\Omega)\to L_2(\gamma\times(0,T))$ and the solution of equation (5) will be searched for in the least-squares formulation:

$$\phi_*(x,y)=\arg\min\left\|\mathcal{A}\phi(x,y)-\xi(s,t)\right\|_{L_2(\gamma\times(0,T))}$$

In [43], by means of a standard technique of embedding theorems, it was proved that the operator A is compact, but does not possess a bounded inverse. Therefore, any attempt to solve equation (5) numerically must be followed by some regularization procedure. In this chapter, a regularization is performed by means of the truncated SVD that leads to a notion of r-solution (see [39]).

4 r-solution

Shortly the notion of r-solution can be described as follows. It is known [44, Ch. IX] that any linear compact operator possesses a matrix representation, and the operator equation (5) can be rewritten as an infinite system of linear algebraic equations. It is also known that any compact operator is represented by a singular system $\{s_j,\vec{u}_j,\vec{v}_j\}$, $j=1,2,\cdots,\infty$, where $s_j\geq 0$, $s_1\geq s_2\geq...\geq s_j\geq...$ are singular values and $\vec{u}_j$ and $\vec{v}_j$ – left and right singular vectors. A very important property of the singular vectors is that they form bases in the data and model spaces, that is, any functions $\varphi(x,y) \in W_2^1(\Omega)$ and $\xi(s,t) \in L_2(\gamma \times (0,T))$ can be presented as the Fourier series:

$$\varphi(x,y) = \sum_{j=1}^{\infty} \varphi_j \vec{v}_j; \quad \xi(s,t) = \sum_{i=1}^{\infty} \xi_i \vec{u}_i; \tag{6}$$

with $\varphi_j = (\varphi(x,y) \cdot \vec{v}_j(x,y))$ and $\xi_i = (\xi(s,t) \cdot \vec{u}_i(t))$. Taking into account these properties one can rewrite equation (5) in the "diagonal" form:

$$\mathcal{A}\left(\sum_{j=1}^{\infty} \varphi_j \vec{v}_j\right) \equiv \sum_{j=1}^{\infty} s_j \varphi_j \vec{u}_j = \sum_{i=1}^{\infty} (\xi(s,t) \cdot \vec{u}_i) u_i \equiv \sum_{i=1}^{\infty} \xi_i \vec{u}_i \tag{7}$$

and its solution is given by

$$\varphi(x,y) = \sum_{j=1}^{\infty} \frac{(\xi(s,t) \cdot \vec{u}_j)}{s_j} \vec{v}_j(x,y). \tag{8}$$

This solution is nothing but the normal general solution and the operator given by the right-hand side of (8) is the normal general pseudoinverse for the operator A (see [46]). As one can see from (8), the ill-posedness of the first kind operator equation with a compact operator is due to the fact that $s_j \to 0$ as $j \to 0$. Therefore, a small perturbation $\varepsilon(t)$ on the right-hand side $\xi(s,t)$ can lead to a rather large perturbation in the solution. It should be noted that the operator perturbation also leads to solution instability. The regularization procedure based on truncated SVD leads to the following notion of r-solution based on the relation:

$$\varphi^{[r]}(x,y) = \sum_{j=1}^{r} \frac{(\xi(s,t) \cdot \vec{u}_j)}{s_j} \vec{v}_j(x,y). \tag{9}$$

The r-solution is the projection of the exact solution on the subspace spanned by the r right singular vectors corresponding to the top singular values of the compact operator A. This truncated series is stable for any fixed parameter r with respect to perturbations of the right-hand side and operator itself (see [44]). It is reasonable that the larger r, the more informative the solution obtained. Finally, the value of r is determined by the singular spectrum and the data noise level.

5 Discretization of the problem

Any numerical method to solve (5) requires a finite-dimensional approximation. Since the operator A is compact, any finite-dimensional approximation, by a $K \times L$ matrix will converge to the operator, as $K, L \to \infty$ and also, $\varphi(x,y)^{KL} \to \varphi(x,y)$ (if it exists). Convergence of the r-solution of a finite-dimensional system of linear algebraic equations to the r-solution of an operator equation was carefully investigated in [44]. Let the domain Ω be a rectangle $[x_1, x_M] \times [y_1, y_N]$. In order to obtain a system of linear algebraic equations by means of a projective method, a trigonometric basis was chosen in the model space, that is, the unknown function $\varphi(x,y)$ has been represented as a series of spatial harmonics

$$\{\varphi_k(x,y) = \sin\frac{m\pi}{l_1}(x - x_c)\cdot\sin\frac{n\pi}{l_2}(y - y_c),$$

$$k = m\cdot n, n = 1,2,\cdots,N, m = 1,2,\cdots,M\}$$

with unknown coefficients $\{c_{mn}\}$:

$$\varphi(x,y) = \sum_{m=1}^{M}\sum_{n=1}^{N}c_{mn}\sin\frac{m\pi}{l_1}(x - x_c)\cdot\sin\frac{n\pi}{l_2}(y - y_c), \tag{10}$$

where

$$l_1 = (x_M - x_1); \quad l_2 = (y_N - y_1), \quad x_c = (x_1 + x_M)/2; \quad y_c = (y_1 + y_N)/2;$$

To sample the necessary data, consider an observation system of P receivers located at points (x_p, y_p), $p = 1,\ldots,P$. In this chapter, the free-surface oscillations $\eta_0(x_p, y_p, t)$ are assumed to be known for a finite number of times $\{t_j\}, j = 1,\ldots,N_t$ at each receiver. It is reasonable to choose a basis in the data space as a system of P vectors $\{\psi_l^{pj} = \delta_{lj}, l = p\cdot j, j = 1,\ldots,N_t, p = 1,\ldots,P\}$. From this, the dimensions of the solution and the data space are

$$\dim(\text{sol}) = K = M\times N; \qquad \dim(\text{data}) = L = P\times N_t;$$

Let us introduce a rectangular grid for the spatial variables and time. A uniform rectangular grid is defined in Π, with some grid points on the dry land. However, our difference scheme employs only grid points located in Φ. It seems more convenient to use the finite difference scheme not for equation (1) but for its equivalent first-order linear system in the unknown water elevation $\eta(x,y,t)$ and the velocity vector $(\zeta(x,y,t),\varsigma(x,y,t))$:

$$\zeta_t + g\eta_x = 0$$
$$\varsigma_t + g\eta_y = 0 \tag{11}$$
$$\eta_t + (h\zeta)_x + (h\varsigma)_y = 0$$

with initial conditions:

$$\eta\mid_t = 0 = \varphi(x,y), \qquad \zeta\mid_t = 0; \quad \varsigma\mid_t = 0. \tag{12}$$

We introduce the rectangular grid with the step Δx, Δy over the spatial variables and Δt over the time. Problems (11) and (12), boundary conditions (3) and condition (4) are approximated by an explicit–implicit finite four-point difference scheme on a uniform rectangular grid [15]. The scheme is of second-order accuracy with respect to the spatial variables and of first order with respect to time. The scheme is based on the so-called spaced pattern, which in combination with central-difference approximation of spatial derivatives simplifies the numerical implementation of boundary conditions, as there is no need to define all the unknown functions on the boundary. As was mentioned earlier, the arrival of the wave on the coast is not considered in this chapter. Simulating the tsunami wave, we need approximation of two types of boundary conditions: (a) conditions on the coastal boundary are assumed to be the full reflection conditions; these are expressed by nullifying the derivative of $\eta(x,y,t)$ with respect to the external normal vector (3); (b) conditions on the so-called free boundaries due to an artificial restriction of a considered domain – the absorbing boundary conditions (ABC). In this chapter, we use the full absorbing conditions of second order of accuracy [47].

As a result the following system of linear algebraic equations in the unknown coefficients $\{c_k = c_{mn}, k = m \cdot n, n = 1,\cdots,N, m = 1,\cdots,M\}$ is obtained:

$$A\tilde{c} = \tilde{b} \tag{13}$$

where

$$\tilde{b} = (\eta_{11}, \eta_{12}, \ldots, \eta_{1N_t}, \eta_{21}, \ldots, \eta_{2N_t}, \eta_{P1}, \ldots, \eta_{PN_t})^T;$$

$$\eta_{pj} = \eta_0(x_p, y_p, t_j), p = 1, \ldots, P, j = 1, \ldots, N_t.$$

To obtain the matrix A, we solve numerically the direct problem (11), (12), and (3) where each of the basic function $\{\varphi_k\}$ is used instead of $\varphi(x,y)$. The matrix A is rectangular with SVD decomposition $A = U\Sigma V^T$, where $\dim(V) = K \times K$ and $\dim(U) = L \times L$. The right singular vectors $\{\tilde{V}_k, k=1,\ldots,K\}$ of the matrix A are columns of the matrix V, the left singular vectors $\{\tilde{U}_i, i=1,\ldots,L\}$ are columns of the matrix U. Following (9) the vector $\tilde{c}$ is sought as the **r**-solution of system (13) in the form:

$$\tilde{c}^{[r]} = \sum_{k=1}^{r} \frac{(\tilde{b}, \tilde{U}_k)}{s_k} \tilde{V}_k(x,y). \tag{14}$$

Then function $\varphi(x,y)$ is obtained as

$$\varphi(x,y)^{[r]} = \sum_{k=1}^{r} \frac{(\tilde{b}, \tilde{U}_k)}{s_k} \tilde{V}_k(x,y), \tag{15}$$

where $\tilde{V}_k(x,y) = \sum_{l=1}^{L} v_{kl} \varphi_l(x,y)$. The number r is taken as

$$r = \max\{k : \frac{s_k}{s_1} \geq \frac{1}{cond}\}, \tag{16}$$

where s_j are the singular values, and cond is the condition number of the matrix A, $s_k \geq 0$, $s_1 \geq s_2, \geq \ldots \geq s_k \geq \ldots$. It is clear that the properties of the matrix A and, consequently, the quality of the obtained solution are determined by the location and extent of the tsunamigenic area, configuration of the observation system, and the temporal extent of the signal. Therefore, the singular spectrum obtained allows one to predict the potential result of reconstruction of the function $\varphi(x,y)$. For example, if the perturbation on the right-hand side $\vec{b}(s,t)$ can be written in the form

$$\vec{\varepsilon}(t) = \sum_{j=1}^{L} \varepsilon_j(t)\vec{U}_j,$$

then the solution will take the form

$$\phi(x,y) = \sum_{k=1}^{K} \frac{b_k + \varepsilon_k}{s_k} \vec{V}_k.$$

In this case the perturbation in the solution has the form

$$\vec{\delta} = \sum_{k=1}^{K} \frac{\varepsilon_k}{s_k} \vec{V}_k.$$

It is clear that $s_j / \varepsilon_j \to 0$ as far as $s_j \to 0$ if $j \to \infty$ and it is necessary to limit the number of used basic vectors proceeding from the cond of a matrix was not very much. While carrying out numerical calculations only right-hand singular vectors with sequence numbers k agreeing with the relation $s_k / s_1 \geq d$ were used. So, the number r is defined from (16), where $d = 1/\text{cond}$ was set in advance. It has been turned out that r, the number of right singular vectors used, is much less than the minimum of the matrix dimensions. The number r depends both on the singular spectrum of the matrix A and on the noise level of the signals observed.

6 Numerical experiments: description and discussion

A series of calculations was made by the proposed method aimed at recovering the unknown function $\varphi(x,y)$:

$$\varphi(x,y) = \beta(x,y) \cdot a(x), \tag{17}$$

where $a(x) = (x - x_0 + 3 * R_1) * (x - x_0 + R_1 / 6)$, and the function $\beta(x,y)$ describes a paraboloid:

$$\beta(x,y) = \begin{cases} 1 - \dfrac{(x-x_0)^2}{R_1^2} - \dfrac{(y-y_0)^2}{R_2^2} & , if \; \dfrac{(x-x_0)^2}{R_1^2} + \dfrac{(y-y_0)^2}{R_2^2} < 1 \\[4mm] 0 & , if \; \dfrac{(x-x_0)^2}{R_1^2} + \dfrac{(y-y_0)^2}{R_2^2} \geq 1. \end{cases}$$

Function $\varphi(x,y)$ (initial sea surface displacement) is in accord with a sea floor deformation of typical tsunamigenic earthquakes with reverse dip-slip or low-angle trust mechanisms.

The main goal of numerical experiments presented in the following was to analyze the influence of the observation system on the quality of the recovering of the initial tsunami waveform. First, the purpose was to obtain the acceptable result of the recovering with the minimum number of the used receivers. It is necessary to recognize that the results obtained strongly depend on the presence of disturbance since the problem is ill-posed. However, since a tsunami wave is usually a low-frequency wave packet (compared to the background noise), it is reasonable enough to apply frequency filtration of the observed signal (or synthetic marigrams in our case). An initial data smoothing was performed by using a method of grid function smoothing proposed by Tsetsoho and Belonosov (see [48, Ch. 3.3]). The idea of the original algorithm was to sew n-times differentiable local approximations of a grid function by the Partition of Unity Method. We made an appropriate two-dimensional-smoothing procedure (based on the aforementioned method) for the recovered tsunami waveform. In all calculations, the quality of the solution strongly depends on the number of receivers and their disposition and is evaluated as the relative errors (in the L_2-norm) for the source function.

In order to avoid influence of other factors, we supposed that the ocean depth is the function of one variable and it is equal to the distance from the coast. This assumption for the function $h(x,y)$ is in good agreement with the bottom topography of the Kuril–Kamchatka shelf zone. All sizes are measured in kilometers. The domain Ω was a rectangle of size $[100; 200] \times [50; 150]$; the center point of the tsunami source was $(x_c; y_c) = (150;100)$. Function $\varphi(x,y)$ was approximately sought for in form (10), where $M = 25$; $N = 11$, $R_1 = 25; R_2 = 50; \phi_m ax \approx 0.73m$. The receivers were disposed in the interval $[10;190]$ of the y-axis (the coastal line), the maximum number of them was $P = 19$. Let us say that this data set defines Model 1.

In Fig. 2 results of the inversion using 2, 3, and 5 marigrams are presented. Matrix A (as a real matrix) is of size 153×275 in the case of three receivers, and 255×275 in the case of five, with that in both cases cond $A > 100$. The marigrams were obtained as a result of solving the direct problem (11)–(12) with boundary conditions (3), perturbed by the background noise, that is, a high-frequency disturbance. In Model 1, all experiments presented here were made with the disturbance rate of 5% of maximum amplitude of the signal over all receivers.

In Fig. 3 relative errors (in L_2-norm) of the recovering of source function for Model 1 using two, three, and five receivers, as functions of receivers disposition, noise levels, and value of cond are presented.

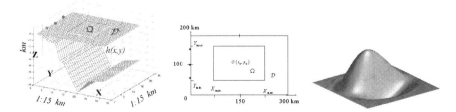

Figure 1: Model 1.

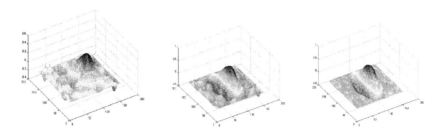

Figure 2: Recovered initial tsunami wave forms by the inversion using 2, 3, and
5 marigrams correspondingly for the numerical Model 1.

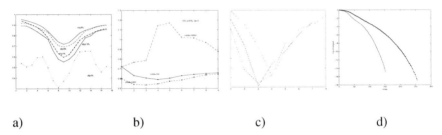

a)   b)   c)   d)

Figure 3: the relative errors (in L_2-norm) of the recovering source functions for
Model 1 with (a) two, (b) three, and (c) five receivers and singular values
for the cases with (d) three and five receivers.

Namely, the curves in Fig. 3(a) show relative errors for the case when two
receivers were used with different levels of the background noise and cond of the
matrix A: 0%, cond = 10^5 – red line; 5%, cond = 10^2 – blue line; 5%, cond = 10^3 –
orange line; 2.5%, cond = 10^3 – green line; 1%, cond = 10^2 – brown line. Location
of the first receiver was fixed at the initial point of the aperture (0,1), the second
one was moved to the endpoint of the coastal segment with coordinates respectively (0, n). By the midpoint we mean the projection of the central point of the
rectangle Ω (or the central point of the source, that is the same) onto the coastal
line. Figure 2.3(b) corresponds to the case when there are three receivers positioned symmetrically with respect to the midpoint of the coast. In all experiments
the horizontal axis points ($n = 1,...9$) were at the distance of $n \times 10\ km$ from the
midpoint to the first supplemental pair of the receivers. The presence of a receiver
in the midpoint has an essential influence on the results because the signal in this
direction is mostly informative. It is typical for all calculations. Increasing of the
cond implies increasing of the r-value and, hence, also informativeness of the solution. However, large oscillations appear in the numerical solution when cond is
excessively large. The proposed approach allows one to control the accuracy by
choosing the appropriate r-value. In Fig. 2.3(c) the relative errors are presented in
the case of using five receivers in the following configuration: one plus two pairs.
One of the receivers was also disposed at the midpoint while two pairs moved symmetrically to the endpoints of the coastal segment while the distance in every pair

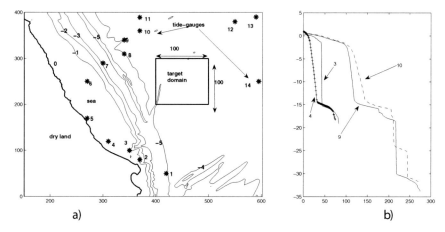

a)   b)

Figure 4: (a) Isolines of the Peru subduction zone with depth values, the target
domain and the fourteen receivers marked by (*); (b) four graphs of singular values of the matrix A on a common log scale depending on their
numbers. The numbers 3, 4, 9, 10 stand for the numbers of receivers used
in certain appropriate variants of reconstruction.

is fixed this distance equals to 40 km (dashed line), 20 km (solid line), and 10 km
(dashed-dot line). It is clear, that each of the represented lines has a point of the
minimum value. In Fig. 3(d) natural logarithms of the singular values are presented
for the cases of three and five receivers for Model 1.

The next data set Model 2 corresponds to the Peru coastal zone: as the function
$h(x,y)$, the real Peru subduction zone was used. The domain Φ was the aquatic part of
the rectangle $\Pi = \{0 \leq x \leq 600; 0 \leq y \leq 400\}$ with piecewise-linear boundaries of dry
land, the domain $\Omega = \{400 \leq x \leq 500; 200 \leq y \leq 300\}$ was a rectangle, see Fig. 4(a),
the center point of a tsunami source was $(x_0; y_0) = (450;250)$, $R_1 = 40$; $R_2 = 50$ (all
sizes are measured in kilometers). The maximum and minimum values of the func-
tion $\varphi(x,y)$ were $\varphi_{max} = 1.959$ m; $\varphi_{min} = -0.67$ m. $M = 25$; $N = 11$ were used in
(10). $\Delta x = \Delta y = 1$ km were the space steps; hence, the domain Ω contained 100×100
mesh points. The time step was $\Delta t = 0.5sec$. Fourteen points in the domain Φ were
chosen as receivers in the numerical experiments, thus $P = 14$. The time interval was
taken large enough so that the tsunami wave reached all the chosen receivers, particularly, number of time steps was $N_t = 1684$. Hence, the following values of K and
L: $K = 25 \cdot 11 = 275$, $L = 14 \cdot 1684$ were used. After specifying all the parameters the
first step of numerical modeling was the calculation of synthetic marigrams in all
receivers by solving the direct problem (11)–(12), (3) with $\varphi(x,y)$ from (17). Thus,
the vector b in (13) was calculated. The second step was to calculate matrix A and
then SVD decomposition by using a standard procedure. Thus, the singular spectrum
that played a key role in estimating the quality of the reconstruction was obtained.

A series of calculations was carried out by the method proposed above to find a
correspondence between certain characteristics of the observation system (such as,

e.g., the number and location of receivers) and results of the reconstruction process. Figure 4 shows (a) contour lines of the real bottom topography of the Peru subduction zone with depth values, the target domain and the 14 receivers enumerated clockwise and marked by (*); (b) typical graphs of common logarithms of singular values of matrix A depending on their numbers. The numbers 3, 4, 9, 10 stand for the numbers of receivers used in certain appropriate variants of reconstruction.

A sharp decrease in the singular values, when their number increases, is typical for all calculations, due to the ill-posedness of the problem. The parameter r in (14) is taken only from an interval, where the common logarithms of singular values are slightly sloping. It follows from Fig. 4(b) that only the number $r = 42$ was suitable for numerical modeling in appropriate variant with three receivers, that is, $P = 3$ and the number $r = 115$ can be used for the reconstruction with 10 receivers ($P = 10$). The performed numerical experiments show that using $r \leq 50$ will not produce an acceptable result. Comparison of the curves for three and four receivers show that the maximum allowable r (as well as properties of the matrix A) depends not only on the quantity of the receivers, but also on their azimuthal coverage. This dependence was investigated in detail in [48]. From the numerical experiments it is clear that a satisfactory parameter value is $r \geq 70$. Analysis of the singular spectrum of the matrix A can be extremely helpful for evaluating the real effectiveness of the tide gauges system for reconstructing the initial water displacement.

In the numerical calculations presented above the r-solution was obtained with cond ≥ 1000. The Table 1 shows how the configuration of the observation system affects the accuracy of tsunami source reconstruction. Here P is the quantity of receivers used in reconstruction; d is log(1/cond); err is the relative error (in the L_2 norm) of the reconstructed function; f max, f min are the extreme values of the function recovered. The last column shows the number of receivers used in the reconstruction in the order of increasing indices, according to Fig. 4.

Table 1: Influence of the observation system configuration, cond A and number r on the accuracy of the tsunami source reconstruction.

P	d	r	err	$f$max (m)	$f$min (m)	Number of receivers
	2	73	0.3767	1.559	−0.717	3, 4, 5, 6, 9, 10, 11
	2	55	0.4436	1.381	−0.768	2, 3, 4, 5, 6, 9, 10
	2	65	0.4588	1.449	−0.923	5, 6, 7, 8, 9, 10, 11
	3	93	0.3164	1.732	−0.6472	5, 6, 7, 8, 9, 10, 11
	4	99	0.2671	1.816	−0.7028	5, 6, 7, 8, 9, 10, 11
	2	42	0.552	1.276	−0.6745	1, 3, 5, 7 ,9 ,11, 13
	4	59	0.3173	1.706	−0.7371	1, 3, 5, 7, 9, 11, 13
	2	23	0.6278	1.106	−0.6959	3, 4, 5, 6, 7, 8, 9
	2	45	0.5752	1.431	−1.35	1, 2, 3, 5, 8, 9, 10
	2	66	0.6443	1.995	−1.920	1, 2, 3, 5, 9, 10, 11

In Fig. 5 the results of reconstructing of the function $\varphi(x, y)$ are presented for the inversion with nine marigrams for different groups of receivers and conditioning numbers of matrix A.

Synthetic marigrams were obtained by solving the direct problem (11)–(12), and (3) perturbed by a background noise. All experiments presented here were carried out with a noise rate of 3% of signal's maximal amplitude over all receivers. In Fig. 6 the initial and the recovered tsunami waveforms are presented.

The next step was solving the direct problem with the recovered and smoothed initial tsunami waveform to calculate marigrams at the same points as the synthetic ones. The results are presented in Fig. 3.

Each of the 14 pictures correspond to the receiver with the same number (see the location of receivers in Fig. 4). Some of the pictures presented here correspond to receivers used in reconstruction, but others correspond to the receivers which were not used called "rest." This means that the synthetic marigrams from the "rest" receivers were not used in formula (4), but the marigrams from the reconstructed tsunami source were calculated at these points. Denote (a) numerical reconstruction

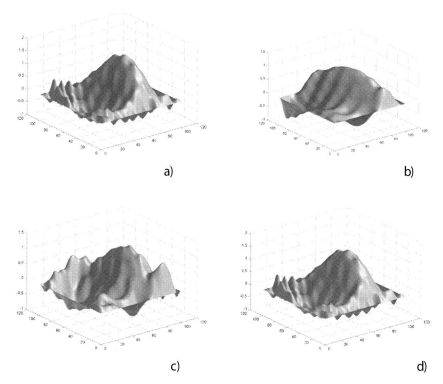

a)   b)

c)   d)

Figure 5: Reconstructed wave forms with nine receivers (a) receivers were used 3, 4, 5, 6, 7, 8, 9, 10, 11; cond = 1000; (b)receivers were used 2, 3, 4, 6, 7, 8, 12, 13, 14; cond = 1000; (c) receivers were used 3, 4, 5, 8, 9, 10, 11, 12, 13; cond = 1000.

Figure 6: Wave forms (a) initial $\varphi_{\max} = 1.959$ m; $\varphi_{\min} = -0.67$ m ; (b) three receivers, $\varphi_{\max} = 1.213(0.885)m$; $\varphi_{\min} = -0.738(-0.357)m$; $r = 41$; err. $= 0.717$; (c) five receivers, $\varphi_{\max} = 1.757(1.4716)m$; $\varphi_{\min} = -1.0073(-.5142)m$; $r = 57$; err. $= 0.4729$; (d) seven receivers, $\varphi_{\max} = 1.835(1.5138)m$; $\varphi_{\min} = -0.7016(-0.5484)m$; err. $= 0.262$; $r = 103$; $\log(1/\text{cond}) = 6$. The values in parentheses are extreme values of the reconstructed waveforms after smoothing.

of a tsunami source by five marigrams from the receivers numerated as 3, 4, 6, 7, 10 as Model 2.1; (b) numerical reconstruction of a tsunami source by seven marigrams from the receivers numerated as 5, 6, 7, 8, 9, 10, 11 as Model 2.2. Every picture contains three graphs: the solid line denotes the synthetic marigram, the dashed line denotes the *marigram* for Model 2.1, and the dash-dotted line denotes the *marigram* for Model 2.2. One can see that Model 2.1 does not match sufficiently the marigrams. On the contrary, Model 2.2 gives a good agreement both for the receivers used in reconstruction and to the "rest" ones. This fact is very significant for the evaluation of the inverse algorithm. For predicting the water elevation in some area on the basis of data provided by some tide gauges the matching of marigrams is more important than the accuracy of reconstruction of a tsunami source. Our approach includes the following steps (1) calculation of the synthetic tide gauge records from a model tsunami source (2) reconstruction of the original tsunami waveform in the target domain by the inversion of marigrams; (3) calculation of the synthetic marigrams from the reconstructed source; (4) determining the most informative part of the observation system for a target area, for example, by comparing the marigrams obtained during previous steps in the same points; 5) setting up the observation system that contains only good-matching stations and reconstructing the tsunami source again, now using only these *nice* tide-gauge records. Obtained after step 5 improved tsunami source can be proposed for use in further tsunami modeling (tsunami wave propagation modeling, etc.).

7 Conclusion

In this chapter, a methodology was proposed for reconstructing initial tsunami waveforms in a tsunami source area based on remote measurements of water-level data. The approach is raised on SVD and r-solutions techniques, which are combined with a smoothing procedure to filter both the initial data and the reconstructed tsunami waveform. By analyzing the characteristics of a given tide gauges network, the above-proposed method allows one to control numerical instability of the solution and therefore to obtain an acceptable result in spite of the ill-posedness of the problem. The algorithm was verified by numerical simulating with real bathymetry of the Peru subduction zone and synthetic data. It has been

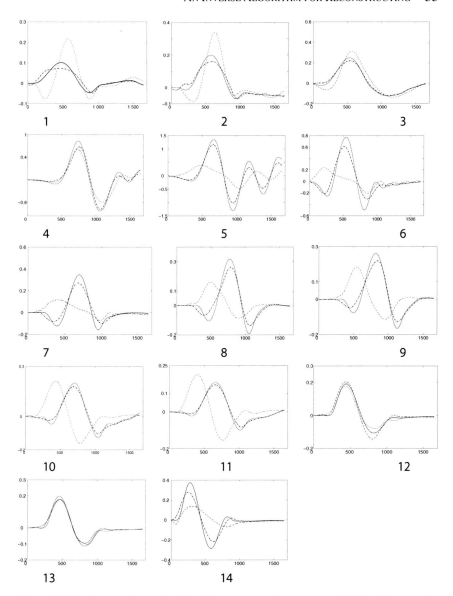

Figure 7: Marigrams in each of the fourteen receivers: the solid line denotes the synthetic marigram, the dashed line denotes the marigram for Model 1 (3, 4, 6, 7, 10 are the number of receivers); the dash-dotted denotes the marigram for Model 2 (5, 6, 7, 8, 9, 10, 11 are the number of receivers used). The horizontal axis is time, the vertical axis is tsunami wave height (*m*).

found out, that the accuracy of tsunami source reconstruction strongly depends on the signal-to-noise ratio, the azimuthal and temporal coverage of assimilated tide gauge stations relative to the target area and the bathymetric features along the wave path. The results thus obtained show that initial tsunami waveform reconstruction by the technique presented in this chapter has been successful.

Acknowledgements

This work was supported by the Russian Foundation for Basic Research under grant No 12-07-00406, by the Siberian Branch of the RAS (Project 117), by the Siberian Branch and the Far-Eastern Branch of the RAS Project 37), by the Ministry of Education and Science of Russian Federation (No. 16.740.11.0057).

References

[1] Abe, K., Tsunami propagation on a seismological fault model of the 1952 Kamchatka earthquake, *Bulletin of Nippon Dental University*, 8, pp. 3–11, 1979.

[2] Aida, I., Numerical computation of a tsunami based on a fault origin model of an earthquake, *Journal of the Seismological Society of Japan*, **27**, pp. 141–154, 1974.

[3] Mader, C.L., Numerical simulation of tsunamis. *Journal of Physical Oceanography*, **4(1)**, pp. 74–82, 1974.

[4] Bernard, E.N., A tsunami research plan for the United States. *Earthquake Engineering Research Institute*, **17**, pp. 13–26, 1983.

[5] Satake, K., Inversion of tsunami waveforms for the estimation of a fault heterogeneity: method and numerical experiments. *Journal of Physics of the Earth*, **35**, pp. 241–254, 1987.

[6] Satake, K., Inversion of tsunami waveforms for the estimation of hereogeneous fault motion of large submarine earthquakes: the 1968 Tokachi-oki and the 1983 Japan sea earthquake. *Journal of Geophysical Research*, **94**, pp. 5627–5636, 1989.

[7] Gonzalez, F.I., Bernard, S.N. & Milbern, H.B., et al., The Pacific Tsunami Observation Program (PacTOP). Proc. IUGG/IOC, Intern. Tsunami Simp., pp. 3–19, 1987.

[8] Titov, V.V. & Synolakis, C.E., Numerical modeling of tidal wave runup. *Journal of Waterway, Port, Coastal and Ocean Engineering*, **124(4)**, 157–171, 1998.

[9] Titov,V.V., Gonzalez, F.I., Bernard, S.N, Eble, M.C., Mofjeld, H.O., Newman, J.C.,& Venturato, A.J., Real-time tsunami forecasting: challenges and solutions. *Natural Hazards*, **35(1)**, Special Issue, US National Tsunami Hazard Mitigation Program, pp. 41–58, 2005.

[10] Tinti, S., Piatanesi, A. & Bortolucci, E., The finite-element wave propagator approach and the tsunami inversion problem, *Journal of Physics and Chemistry of the Earth*, **12**, pp. 27–32, 1996.

[11] Soloviev, S.L., The tsunami problem and its significance for the Kamchatka and the Kuril islands (in Russian), The Tsunami problem, Nauka, Moscow, pp.7–50, 1968.

[12] Gusyakov, V.K. & Chubarov, L.B., Numerical modeling of generation and propagation of tsunami in coastal zone, Izvestiya, Physics of the Solid Earth, **23(11)**, pp. 53–64, 1987.

[13] Chubarov, L.B. & Fedotova, Z.I., Numerical simulation of the long-wave runup on a coast. *Russian Journal of Numerical Analysis and Mathematical Modelling*, **18(2)**, pp. 135–158, 2003.

[14] Shokin, Yu.I., Chubarov, L.B., Fedotova, Z.I., Beizel, S.A. & Eletsky, S.V., Principles of numerical modeling applied to the tsunami problem. *Russian Journal of Earth Sciences*, American Geophysical Union, The World Publishing Service, 8, ES6004, doi: 10.2205/2006ES000216. ISSN: 1681-1208 (online), p. 23, 2006.

[15] Marchuk, An.G., Chubarov, L.B. & Shokin, Yu. I., *The Numerical Simulation of the Tsunami Wave*, Nauka Publishing House: Novosibirsk, pp. 369, 1983.

[16] Fedotova, Z.I. & Khakimzyanov, G.S., Nonlinear- dispersive shallow water equations on a rotating sphere. *Russian Journal of Numerical Analysis and Mathematical Modelling*. VNU Science Press BV, **25(1)**, pp. 15–26, 2010.

[17] Shokin, Y.I. & Chubarov, L.B. , Novikov, V.A. & Sudakov, A.N., Calculations of tsunami travel time charts in the Pacific Ocean - models, algorithms, techniques, results. *Science of Tsunami Hazards*, **5**, pp. 85–113, 1987.

[18] HTDB/WLD (2012), Historical Tsunami Database for the World Ocean (2012), Web-version is available at http://tsun.sscc.ru/nh/tsunami.php.

[19] Goto, C., Ogava, Y., & Imamura, F., Numerical method of tsunami simulation with the leap-frog scheme, (English translation and preparation by N. Shuto), in IUGG/IOC Time Project, IOC Manual and Guides, UNESCO, Paris 35, p. 126, 1997.

[20] Kurkin, A., Zaitsev, A., Yalciner, A. & Pelinovsky, E. Modified computer code "TSUNAMI" forevaluation of risks connected to tsunami. *Izvestia, Russian Academy of Engineering Sciences, Series: AppliedMathematics and Mechanics*, **9**, pp. 88–100, 2004.

[21] Titov, V.V. & Gonzalez, F.I., Implementation and Testing of The Method of Splitting Tsu-nami (MOST) Model, NOAA Technical Memorandum ERL PMEL-112, p. 11, 1997.

[22] Okada, Y., Surface deformation due to shear and tensile faults in a half-space. *Bulletin of the Seismological Society of America*, **75(4)**, pp. 1135–1154, 1985.

[23] Eletsky, S.V., Fedotova, Z.I. & Chubarov, L.B., Computer model of tsunami waves, *Proc. of Tenth Baikal All Russia Conf., Information and Mathematical Technologies in Science, Technology, and Education*, Part 1, ISEM, p. 138, 2005.

[24] Nwogu, O., Alternative form of Boussinesq equations for near shore wave propagation. *Journal of Waterway, Port, Coastal and Ocean Engineering.*, **119(6)**, pp. 618–638, 1993.

[25] Lynett, P. & Liu P.L.F., A numerical study of submarine landslide gener- ated waves and runup. *Proceedings of the Royal Society of London,* **458**, pp. 2885–2910, 2002.

[26] Pelinovsky, E.N., Tsunami Wave Hydrodynamics, Institute Applied Physics Press, Nizhny Novgorod, 1996 (in Russian).

[27] Wei, G. & Kirby, J.T., A time-dependent numerical code for extended Boussi- nesq equations. *Journal of Waterway, Port, Coastal, and Ocean Engineering,* **121**, pp. 251–261, 1995.

[28] Watts, P. & Grilli, S.T., Underwater landslide shape, motion, deformation, and tsunami generation , *Proc. of the 13th Offshore and Polar Engr. Conf.,* ISOPE03, Honolulu, Hawaii, 3, pp. 364–371, 2003.

[29] Watts, P., Grilli, S.T., Kirby, J.T., Fryer, G. J. & Tappin, G.R., Landslide tsunami case studies using a Boussinesq model and a fully nonlinear tsu- nami generation model. Natural Hazards and Earth Systems Sciences, **3**, pp. 391–402, 2003.

[30] Shokin, Yu.I., Babailov, V.V., Beisel, S.A., Chubarov, L.B., Eletsky, S.V., Fedo-tova, Z.I. & Gusiakov, V.K., Mathematical Modeling in Application to Regional Tsunami Warning Systems, Operations, Comp. Science and High Perf. Computing III, NNFM, Springer-Verlag: Berlin, Heidelberg, 101/2008, pp. 52–68, 2008.

[31] Levin, B.W. & Nosov, M.A., *Physics of Tsunamis*, Springer, p. 327, 2008.

[32] Gusiakov, VK, Yeletsky, S., Fedotova, Z.I. & Chubarov, L.B., Review and comparison of several software systems for simulation of the tsunami, *Proc. of the I(XIX) International Conference of Young Scientists*, devoted to the 60-anniversary of the Institute of Marine Geology and Geophysics FEB RAS, Study of natural catastrophes in Sakhalin and Kuril Islands (in Russia), Yuzhno-Sakhalinsk, pp. 214–221, 2007.

[33] Johnson, J.M.: Heterogeneous coupling along Alaska-Aleutian as inferred from tsunami, seismic and geodetic inversion. *Advances in Geophysics,* **39**, pp. 1–116, 1999.

[34] Johnson, J.M., Satake, K., Holdahl, S.R. & Sauber, J., The 1964 Prince William sound earthquake: joint inversion of tsunami and geodetic data, *Journal of Geophysical Research,* **101**, pp. 523–532, 1996.

[35] Piatanesi, A., Tinti, S. & Pagnoni, G., Tsunami waveform inversion by numerical finite-elements Green's Functions. *Natural Hazards and Earth System Science,* **1**, pp. 187–194, 2001.

[36] Pires, C. & Miranda, P.M.A., Tsunami waveform inversion by adjont meth- ods. *Journal of Geophysical Research,.***106**, pp. 19773–19796, 2001.

[37] Baba, T., Cummins, P.R, Hong Kie, T. & Hiroaki, T., *Validation and Joint Inversion of Teleseismic Waveforms for Earthquake Source Models Using Deep Ocean Bottom Pressure Records: A Case Study of the 2006 Kuril Megathrust Earthquake, Pure and Applied Geophysics*, Vol. 166. Springer, Birkhäuser-Verlag, pp. 55–76, 2009.

[38] Voronina, T. A. & Tcheverda, V.A., Reconstruction of tsunami initial form via level oscillation. *Bulletin of the Novosibirsk Computing Center Series Mathematical Modeling in Geophysics,* **4**, pp. 127–136, 1998.

[39] Cheverda, V.A. & Kostin, V. I., r-pseudoinverse for compact operators in Hilbert space: existence and stability. *Journal of Inverse and Ill-Posed Problems*, **3**, pp. 131–148, 1995.

[40] Kaistrenko, V. M., Inverse problem for reconstruction of tsunami source. *Tsunami Waves, Sakhalin Compl. Inst.Press*, **29**, pp. 82–92, 1972.

[41] Ladyzhenskaya, O.A., *Boundary-Value Problems of Mathematical Physics*. Springer: New York, pp. 407, 1985.

[42] Hormander, L., *The Analysis of Linear Partial Differential Operators*, Springer-Verlag: Berlin, 1983.

[43] Voronina, T, Reconstruction of initial Tsunami waveforms by a truncated SVD method. Journal of Inverse and Ill-posed Problems, **19(4–5)**, pp. 615–629, ISSN (Print) 0928-0219, 2011.

[44] Voronina, T.A., Determination of spatial distribution of oscillation sources by remote measurements on a finite set of points. *Siberian Journal of Numerical Mathematic (SibJNM)*, Since 2008 the English version has been titling '*Numerical Analysis and Applications*' distributed by Springer, **3**, pp. 203–211, 2004.

[45] Kantorovich, L.V. & Akilov, G.P., *Functional Analysis*, Macmillan: New York, p. 650, 1964.

[46] Zuhair Nashed, M., Aspects of generalized inverses in analysis and regularization. *Generalized Inverses and Applications*. Academic Press: New York, pp. 193–244, 1976.

[47] Enquist, B., Majda, A., Absorbing boundary conditions for the numerical simulation of waves, Mathematics of Computation, **139**, pp. 629–654, 1977.

[48] Marchuk, G.I., *Methods of Numerical Mathematics*, Springer-Verlag: New York, Heidelberg, Berlin, p. 493, 1982.

CHAPTER 3

Tsunami maximum flooding assessment in GIS environment

G. Mastronuzzi[1,2], S. Ferilli[3], A. Marsico[1], M. Milella[4],
C. Pignatelli[5], A. Piscitelli[4], P. Sansò[6] & D. Capolongo[1]
[1]*Dip. di Scienze della Terra e Geoambientali, Università degli Studi "Aldo Moro", Via Orabona 4 – 70125 Bari, Italy*
[2]*LAGAT-TA Laboratorio Gis Geo-Ambientale e di Telerilevamento di Taranto, Università degli Studi "Aldo Moro", Polo Jonico, II Facoltà di Scienze MM.FF.NN, Via A. De Gasperi (Paolo VI) – 74100 Taranto, Italy*
[3]*Dip. di Informatica, Università degli Studi "Aldo Moro", Via Orabona 4 – 70125 Bari, Italy*
[4]*Environmental Surveys s.r.l, Via della Croce 156 – 74123 Taranto, Italy*
[5]*Geo Data Service s.r.l, Via della Croce 156 – 74123 Taranto, Italy*
[6]*Dip. di Scienze e Tecnologie Biologiche e Ambientali, Università del Salento, Via per Arnesano, 73100 Lecce, Italy*

Abstract

The presence of mega-boulders scattered landward along gently sloping rocky coasts is attributed to the impact of tsunami or of exceptional storms. Considering the original position and the size of the largest boulder is possible to estimate the characteristics of the wave that moved them in the past, and then estimate the maximum inundation. The present roughness of the coastal area conditions the capacity of the tsunami inland penetration in case of a future event. The knowledge of the parameters of the possible tsunami together with the coastal topography and roughness make possible to estimate automatically scenarios of probable flooding.

1 Introduction

The recent events of Chile (February 27, 2010) and Tohoku Oji tsunamis (March 11, 2011) highlighted the extensive flooding of the coastal area due to their impact.

The implementation of models that simulate the complex processes occurring during inundation allows run-up and flooded area to be assessed and civil protection plans to be realized. The growing concentration of population and human activities in coastal areas, in fact, determines the increase of exposed values and, consequently, rises up hazard, vulnerability and risk. The implementation of the knowledge concerning every significant change of the coastal environment in relation to the increase of human activities and natural evolution allows the construction of predictive models and/or risk assessment.

Deposits consisting of large boulders, isolated or sparse or accumulated in fields and berms, can be recognised frequently along the rocky coast. This geomorphological evidence testifies the impact of extreme waves – tsunamis and/or exceptional storms – occurred in the recent past [1–10]. Recent papers indicated that detailed survey of boulder fields and accumulations (shape, size(s), rock density, etc.) is useful to evaluate the minimum wave height able to detach/move boulders from the circalittoral/adlittoral environments and accumulate them inland. Starting from these features, some formulas have been developed to describe the tsunamis/ storms features and in particular their height, H_T or H_s, respectively [11–16]. Furthermore, the estimation of the minimum wave height allows us to calculate the flooding limit along coasts characterised by flat profile by applying the empirical formula of Hills and Mader [17]:

$$X_{max} = (H_T)^{1.33} n^{-2} k \qquad (1)$$

where H_T is the height of the tsunami to the coastline, n is the Manning coefficient, $k = 0.06$ is a constant that is used for many tsunamis [18]. In most cases, the coastal area is characterized by the sloping profile; hence, it is possible to consider (2) [13]:

$$X_{max} = D + (H_{FL})^{1.33} n^{-2} k \cos \alpha \qquad (2)$$

In this equation, D represents the inland position (distance from the coastline) of the largest boulder displaced by tsunami. H_{FL} is the height of the flood running inland corresponding to $H_T - H_C$ where the latter is the cliff height.

Evidently, the values obtained by (1) and (2) are strongly influenced by the Manning number (n); it takes into account the hydraulic roughness that is a quantification of the resistance that an irregular surface opposes to the water flow in a channel [19, 20]. There are, therefore, different Manning coefficients, depending on the surface features that water flow encounters during its propagation inland (sand, rock, vegetation, buildings, etc.). This parameter is difficult to be quantified if it is not directly measured, but photographic evidence and/or post-event surveys allowed us to correlate classes of surfaces to n values that express their roughness [21]. In every coastal area, the Manning number is not constant over time due to growth of vegetation, processes of coastal weathering, karstification, abrasion and urban development [22]. Numerous studies carried out on open channels in case of flows without lateral boundaries suggest that the roughness of a given surface crossed by a flow can be obtained considering the standard deviation of the bottom and the flow depth [23–25]:

$$n = \frac{k\sqrt[6]{R}}{g} \cdot \frac{1-\left(\dfrac{Z_0}{R}\right)}{\left[\left(\dfrac{Z_0}{R}\right)-\ln\left(\dfrac{Z_0}{R}\right)-1\right]} \tag{3}$$

where k is the constant of Von Karman, g is the gravitational constant, R is the depth of the flow and Z_0 is the standard deviation of the surface bottom. This equation may correspond to the case of flood produced by tsunami(s).

The terrestrial laser scanner (TLS) survey permits to obtain *in situ* measurement of the micro-topography of a surface; this technique supplies a point cloud from which it is possible to reconstruct a digital terrain model (DTM) and the relative standard deviation with a definition of the order of millimetres [26]. The objective of our current researches is to improve a digital tool we recently developed [27]; it, operating in a Geographic Information System (GIS) environment, is able to calculate automatically the limit of inundation due to a tsunami of known height (H_T). Five coastal areas of southern Apulia marked by large limestone and/or calcarenite boulders deposited by tsunami(s) in historical time have been chosen as case study [5, 9, 28, 29] (Fig. 1). Their TLS surveys allow the Nott's equation [11] for the joint bounded scenario to be improved and a new equation aimed at assessing the maximum flooding due to tsunami to be proposed [13].

This work is an attempt to extend to the entire perimeter of Southern Apulia the conclusions obtained in the case study of Torre Castiglione [27]. With this aim, the following steps have been carried out: *(i)* TLS survey to obtain different roughness coefficients as a function of the prevailing surfaces features (coastal karstified

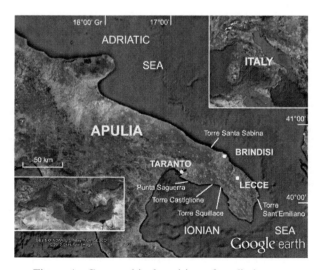

Figure 1: Geographical position of studied areas.

calcarenite, covered karstified calcarenite, sand, vegetation, etc.); *(ii)* assessment of the minimum wave necessary to transport the largest boulder; *(iii)* implementation of an informatic tool that allows the automatic identification and extent of the different types of surface by orthophotos analysis and the definition of flooding area using (2).

2 Coastal geomorphology

The five study areas considered in this work are placed both along the Adriatic side (Torre Santa Sabina, Brindisi) and the Ionian one (Torre Sant'Emiliano and Torre Squillace – Province of Lecce; Torre Castiglione and Punta Saguerra – Province of Taranto) of southern Apulia (Fig. 1). These coastal areas show seaward sloping surfaces, staircase arranged and placed at different elevation above the mean sea level; they are shaped on bioclastic/algal calcarenite except at Torre Sant'Emiliano, where the coast is shaped directly in the Mesozoic limestone that represents the local basement. These surfaces correspond to Middle–Late Pleistocene marine terraces produced by the superimposition of regional uplift and sea level changes [30].

In particular, the local landscape is characterised by sub-horizontal surfaces generally placed between the sea level and 5 m above mean sea level with the exception of Torre Sant'Emiliano, where the lowest marine terrace is placed at about 10 m above mean sea level. Seaward, surfaces are limited by a cliff 4/6 m high, only partly emerged except in Torre Sant'Emiliano locality, where sea bottom is very deep, about 30 m below mean sea level. The adlittoral areas are characterised inland by a standard sequence of *(i)* karstified rock; *(ii)* soil cover; *(iii)* vegetation. The first one is characterised by pinnacles, solution pools and erosive channels due to the combined effect of wave erosion and spray induced karst. The result is a very irregular surface (Fig. 2). Landward a rapid change in the microtopography can be surveyed. This area is the result of soil-stripping

Figure 2: Pinnacles, solution pools and erosive channels define a very irregular surface due to the combined effect of wave erosion and spray induced karst that characterize the adlitoral area near the coastline: (A) algal calcarenite of Punta Saguerra, Taranto (fractures due to the marine undercutting are also readable); (B) algal calcarenite of Torre Castiglione, Taranto; (C) biocalcarenite of Torre Santa Sabina, Brindisi.

phenomena most likely related to the action of exceptional waves (Fig. 3). A vegetated strip follows inland; it is characterised mainly by bushes and low trees in a natural photo-assemblage known as 'macchia mediterranea' [31].

Megaboulders have been found at different distances from the coastlines and elevation on the mean sea level (maximum tidal excursion is of 0.30–0.50 m). At Torre Sant'Emiliano (Fig. 4) and Punta Saguerra (Fig. 5) they are arranged in a complex berm up to 2.5 km long; sparse boulders are recognisable at Torre Santa Sabina (Fig. 6) and at Torre Castiglione (Fig. 7); isolated boulders have been found at Torre Squillace (Fig. 8). The size of the largest boulders ranges from 5.0 × 3.5 × 1.5 m (Torre Sant'Emiliano boulder accumulation) to 3.2 × 2.8 × 1.8 m (Torre Castiglione locality) (Table 1).

Boulders' surface is generally deeply karstified by sea spray; the presence of solution pools and pinnacles on their surface clearly indicates their original position in subaerial environment, close to the coastline. On the other hand, areas from which boulders have been scraped are still recognizable due to the presence of niches of detachment. However, some boulders have been detached from subtidal or intertidal environments as testified by the presence of bio-concretions on their

Figure 3: Flat-like surface due to soil-stripping phenomena related to the impact of exceptional waves at Torre Squillace, Lecce.

Figure 4: The boulders berm of Torre Sant'Emiliano, Lecce.

Figure 5: The boulders berm of Punta Saguerra, Taranto.

Figure 6: The boulders field of Torre Santa Sabina, Brindisi.

Figure 7: The boulders field of Torre Castiglione, Taranto.

Table 1: Synoptical table showing largest boulders features surveyed in the studied areas; JBS: Joint Bounded Scenario [11]; (?) indicate that the date is not sure.

Locality	Elevation (m a.m.s.l.)	Distance from coast-line (m)	a × b × c axis (m)	Rocky density (gr/cm³)	Weight (tons)	Original position	Tsunami Height H_T (m)	Cliff Height H_C (m)	Flooding Height H_{FL} (m)	Tsunami event	Reference
Torre Santa Sabina	1.0	10	2.9 × 2.4 × 0.7	1.62	8	Intertidal JBS	1.5	0.2	1.3	06.06.1667(?) 02.20.1743	[29]
Torre Sant' Emiliano	4.0	15	5.0 × 3.5 × 1.5	2.71	71	Adlittoral JBS	6.9	3.5	3.4	02.20.1743	[5]
Torre Squillace	1.8	40	5.8 × 1.9 × 1.0	2.35	24	Adlittoral JBS	3.6	1.1	2.5	12.05.1456	[28, 33]
Torre Castiglione	3.5	35	3.2 × 2.8 × 1.8	2.33	37	Adlittoral JBS	6.5	2.0	4.5	12.05.1456 (?) 24.04.1836	[2]
Punta Saguerra	5.0	27	3.7 × 3.1 × 1.2	2.20	30	Subtidal JBS	4.1	1.7	2.4	24.04.1836	[9]

Figure 8: The sparse boulders of Torre Squillace, Lecce.

Figure 9: Flooding generated by the storm occurred on January 2002 along the
coast of Santa Sabina, Brindisi.

surfaces [32]. Boulders seem to have never moved in the last 15 years of survey;
the only exception is represented by a boulder 1.4 tons heavy moved in Torre Santa
Sabina locality by the waves of two different storms occurred in the first day of
January 2002 and 2003 (Fig. 9). These storms were the most energetic recognised
in the last 15 years [29].

3 Materials and methods

Data coming from the studied areas have been stored in a GIS based on official
geographical instruments provided by the Administration of Apulia Region. In
particular, the 1:5000 Carta Tecnica Regionale was exploited as a topographic
base on which high resolution orthophotos (0.50 m side grid, 16 million colours)

Figure 10:   Terrestrial laser scanner Leica Scan Station 2 working along the coast
of Marseille, France. On the boulders surfaces targets are recognisable.

have been overlapped. Moreover, a DTM with a resolution of 8 m is associated
with each orthophoto. Documents, orthophoto and DTM relative to the entire
regional coastal perimeter are available at www.sit.puglia.it.

Data derived from the official cartography have been associated with the georeferenced data directly surveyed by TLS by means of a GIS. A Leica Scan Station
2 has been exploited for the TLS survey; it is characterised by a laser generator that
emits pulses in the visible range with maximum frequency of 50,000 points/s up to
a distance of 300 m. It records the reflectance of any surface through two windows
placed one on the front side and the other on the upper one and a servo-motor that
allows the rotation of 360° horizontal and 270° vertically (Fig. 10). The instrument
returns a point cloud oriented in the space that can be georeferenced. Point shows
a different tonality of colour in response to surveyed material reflectivity; the system is also equipped with a digital camera that allows to record the scene by a
single frame (24° × 24° opening with a maximum resolution of 2 Mpixels) automatically aligned [26].

To obtain a three-dimensional representation of the landscape it is necessary to
perform multiple scans from different points of view aiming to eliminate areas not
reached by laser beam. The different scans obtained in this way must be joined
during the post-processing through the spatial alignment of at least three fixed
points (targets) readable from different scan points (Fig. 10). Moreover, the location of the targets and TLS points of view have been acquired by means of a differential GPS Leica GNSS 1250 employed in RTK modality; this device allows
the spatial georeferencing of the three-dimensional point cloud. The Global Navigation Satellite System (GNSS) network of the Apulia region has been used to
obtain the differential correction by means of a GPRS connection.

The collected digital data were managed by Cyclone 6.3 and Rapidform 2006.
The Cyclone package contains three main modules referred to SCAN, REGISTER
and SURVEY. The first allows the acquisition of the point cloud, pictures and

targets; the second one allows us to merge several scans using targets as overlapping points; the third module enables the cleaning of possible outliers from point cloud and imports GPS coordinates. Together these software modules permitted the reconstruction of the three-dimensional view and the sizes assessment.

The three-dimensional reconstruction of the whole area employed TLS provided files ranging from about 2,300,000 to 2,600,000 points, each georeferenced by means of targets coordinates and referred to Gauss-Boaga, Rome 40 datum, zone east. In the Torre Castiglione area, an error of 0.012 m deriving from $dx = 0.008$ m, $dy = 0.002$ and $dz = 0.004$ m [26] has been estimated; in the Punta Saguerra area the entire registration error is 0.027 m deriving from $dx = 0.015$ m, $dy = 0.022$ and $dz = 0.001$ m [27]; in Torre Squillace area the error is about 0.019 m connected to a $dx = 0.011$ m, $dy = 0.005$ and $dz = 0.004$ m.

With respect to step *(i)*, the test has been performed on areas corresponding to the ones represented in the orthophoto and DTM from the Sistema Informativo Territoriale (SIT) of the Apulia region. As regards steep *(ii)*, homogeneous areas based on the classification of land use Corine Land Cover and some lithological classes have been identified and manually defined on the orthophotos.

4 Tsunami height and manning number

TLS survey has been performed on the test areas of Torre Squillace (Lecce), Torre Castiglione (Taranto) and Punta Saguerra (Taranto) aiming to obtain some representative values of the Manning number. This choice is justified by the high degree of preservation of the natural features of the coastal landscape. On the other hand, no data were collected from the areas of Torre Santa Sabina (Brindisi) due to its high degree of urbanisation, and from Torre Sant'Emiliano (Lecce) due to logistic difficulties.

In the studied sites, the use of the TLS allows us to survey a strip some hundred meter wide inland from the shoreline. With the goal to define the flooded area, two steps were considered *(i)* the evaluation of the boulders size aimed to identify the H_T; *(ii)* the evaluation of the Manning numbers aimed to identify the X_{max}.

H_T, the height of tsunami wave, is represented by the water column height reaching the coastline. The rapid sea level rise deriving by tsunami propagation determines processes of erosion, transport and accumulation of debris and sediment; in particular, these last factors determine a change in the viscosity and density of sea water. In our cases, the calculation of the density changes – as well as possible effects of backwash – has been neglected.

As supposed in the case of past tsunamis impact [6, 9] and evidenced in the case of recent ones [4, 34], tsunami is able to carve large boulders from the infralittoral, intertidal, or adlittoral zone and to scatter them at various distances from the coastline. The starting hypothesis is that boulders distribution is a function of the parameters that characterise the impacting wave and their original position. By applying appropriate hydrodynamic equations [11, 13] it is possible to calculate the minimum wave height required to move a boulder originally placed in a joint bounded scenario (JBS), that is, separated from the bedrock by fractures and/or strata planes, but still in its original position. This is the pre-transport condition of boulders reported in Table 1. So, considering this scenario, the minimum wave is

$$H_T = 0.5[c(\rho_b - \rho_w)/\rho_w]/C_L \qquad (4)$$

where c represents the thickness of boulder, ρ_b and ρ_w are, respectively, the densities of the rock that constitutes the boulder and the density of water (1.02 g/ml), $C_L = 0.178$ is the lift coefficient of boulder [35].

Values of minimum tsunami height and height of the flooding column water have been obtained by processing the c-axis and the density of the largest boulders (Table 1). The c-axis value has been determined, thanks to the elaboration of the point clouds obtained by the TLS survey of different boulders (Fig. 11) [33].

Depending on different H_T – derived by boulders scattered inland by different tsunamis, or hypothesized in different possible scenarios – these data permitted to obtain different Manning numbers applying the Smart's formula [24]. To assess the roughness of the Torre Castiglione, Punta Saguerra and Torre Squillace areas

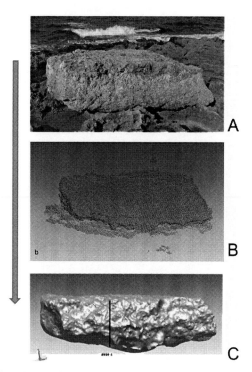

Figure 11: Boulder, TLS point cloud and reconstructed boulder from Torre Santa Sabina, Brindisi. A bio-concrection of *Dendropoma petreum* along the vertical face indicates the original position of the boulder in the intertidal zone.

three different patches of area ranging from 1 × 1 to 10 × 10 m were extrapolated from the TLS point cloud (Fig. 12). They correspond to three different features of the surfaces *(i)* the first is characterized by a very rough surface topography with pinnacles up to about 0.5–1.0 m high, so the flow of sea water that passes through this strip is slowed down both by a horizontal component and by a vertical one; *(ii)* the second is characterized by a homogeneous concave–convex topography, possibly corresponding to an area of cover karst, occasionally covered by sand,

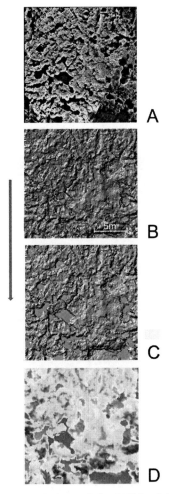

Figure 12: (A) Two-dimensional view of the DEM of the Punta Saguerra point cloud. The black areas correspond to no data shadowed areas. (B) The perimeters of the rockpools are marked by white lines. (C) DEM with rockpool surfaces reconstructed by means of the Rapidform three-dimensional modelling software. (D) Digital reconstruction of the microtopography and slope value.

bare or covered by low vegetation; (iii) the last strip is represented by a thin sand cover completely vegetated.

The three-dimensional point cloud was converted to the interchange file .dxf and imported into an ArcGIS environment for its conversion to shapefile format 3D.shp. The digital terrain model was determined using an interpolation algorithm IDW (Inverse Distance Weighted) with 1 cm size cell. The assumption on which this algorithm is based is that closer objects are more similar than more distant ones. To define values in not measured points, IDW uses the known values in the neighborhood, the nearest known points having a weight greater than the far ones, so that the influence of any known point decreases with distance. The weight assigned to a known point is proportional to the inverse of the distance elevated to a factor p. In their definition, a cross correlation for different ps is activated; for each of these correlations the Root Mean Percentage Scales Error (RMSPE) is calculated; the chosen p is that for which the RMSPE is minimal. Since the weight of a known point decreases rapidly with distance, to speed up computation a maximum number of points on which we perform the calculation is defined.

The next step was the reconstruction of the average shape of the sample area. The applied algorithm, trend, reconstructs the general features of the surface; the operator must indicate the order of the polynomial to be applied, which gives an indication of the surface undulation (1 if the surface is flat; 2 if corrugated; higher values, for more complex shapes). In the case of Torre Castiglione and of Torre Squillace, the surface is quite flat; Punta Saguerra shows a gently slope.

The reconstructed surface is (i) the representative bottom on which the height of the flow is measured; (ii) the reference surface to realize the detrending. The detrending of the DTM is the elimination of the general slope of the surface; it is obtained by subtracting the average shape from the real surface using the raster calculator tool of ArcGIS. The calculated raster surface supplied the value of the standard deviation Z_0 to be used in equation (3). Considering the Smart's formula [24], it is evident that the value of the Manning number is the function of the height of seawater column flooding the coastal area. It is not possible to obtain an absolute value but only a range related to the starting hypothesis, in this case: '... the boulders have been scattered inland by a tsunami of know height...': the effect of slowing due to microtopography characterised by pinnacles 0.50 m high will be different in the case of an impacting wave 1 or 10 m high. Starting from boulder sizes and after deriving the supposed tsunami heights, examples of the obtained data are represented in Tables 2 and 3.

Table 2: Manning numbers obtained in the case of Torre Castiglione, Taranto (from [27]).

Surface	H (m)	R (m)	Z_0	N
Calcarenite	6.5	4.5	0.012526	0.0335
Sand/calcarenite/vegetation	3.7	3.7	0.061348	0.0497
Vegetation	3.1	3.1	0.01788	0.0366

Table 3: Parameters used to define the Manning numbers applying the Smart's formula in the Punta Saguerra, Taranto (from [26]). In this case, different heights of impacting tsunami wave have been considered H; R is the flow height after the impact on the cliff; Z_0 is the related standard deviation of the bottom surface.

Surface	H (m)	R (m)	Z_0	N
Kastified Calcarenite	3	1.04	0.10458	0.0828
Kastified Calcarenite	4	2.04	0.10458	0.0675
Kastified Calcarenite	5	3.04	0.10458	0.0618
Kastified Calcarenite	6	4.04	0.10458	0.0586

5 The flooding area assessment

The prototype system for automatic calculation of tsunami flooding area has been developed using Java language; it runs on both Linux and Windows platforms, and exploits the ImageJ graphics library for image manipulation functionality. It provides the following features (Fig. 13) *(i)* loading of orthophotos (or pre-processed pseudocolour images representing the types of surface) and their associated DTM; *(ii)* identification of homogeneous areas of land and their labelling by type; *(iii)* (automatic) rotation of an orthophoto to make the wavefront perpendicular to the coast impacting; *(iv)* assessment of the flooding with respect to a wave height selected by user.

Starting from the loaded image, the current prototype provides for the identification of regions and their manual labelling from the overlap of these areas on the georeferenced orthophoto. In our case, the various kinds of surfaces were manually identified, represented using different colours according to the Corine Land Use Cover, and imported manually in the GIS; the roughness value, determined from TLS data and the formula of [24], was associated with each type of surface. Studies are ongoing to apply image processing techniques that automatically identify homogenous areas in the orthophoto, and machine learning techniques that learn to automatically classify different types of zones. The main problem is to identify homogeneous areas with sufficient precision, preserving the sharpness of their borders, and to distinguish zones having the same colour or 'structure' in the orthophoto but actually corresponding to different types of surface.

After loading, the image is rotated so that the assumed direction of the supposed impacting tsunami is perpendicular to the general trend of the coastline. The rotation angle can be entered manually or automatically computed by the system. Additionally, an advanced feature that computes the tsunami direction as perpendicular to each single point of the coastline is available. Finally, formula (2) is applied to buffers 1 pixel wide (corresponding to 0.5 m in the available orthophotos, a resolution that would be unfeasible by non-automatic procedures). Excluding sea areas, starting from each coast point and proceeding in the assumed tsunami direction, the system identifies sequences of homogeneous points for the surface

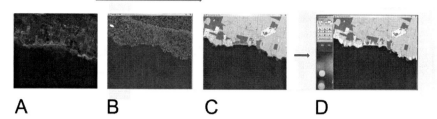

Figure 13: Sequence of the steps necessary to produce the simulation of a flooding
due to a tsunami characterized by $H_T = 6.57$ m [27].

type and altitude, and estimates the hypothetical lowering of the wave in that section according to the associated roughness. Then *(i)* if the wave decreases to zero
within that section, the exact point where it reaches zero is computed and marked
on the map; *(ii)* if the wave height is still larger than zero after traversing that section, its height at the end of the section is computed, and processing goes on to the
next section in that buffer. Special cases (buffers containing only sea areas, where
no flooding can be computed; buffers where the flooding exceeds the visible terri-
tory) are suitably notified.

6 Discussion and conclusions

The model has been applied in two different tests on the coastal area of Torre
Castiglione. In the first case, Manning numbers derived from the literature were
used and a larger number of types of surface manually recognized in the orthophotos were considered. In the second case, the Manning number has been estimated
for a smaller area based on TLS data; classes of surfaces were extracted automatically from the orthophoto. The procedures and results of two different tests are
described in the following.

In the first test, a shapefile TYPE_SURFACE was created with the ArcMap editor, which accurately describes the current land use classes identified in the orthophoto 511101. This shapefile was edited on the geo-referenced orthophotos and
exported from ArcMap as a .png image with the original resolution. Since no TLS
data of the entire portion of landscape represented in the orthophoto are available,
in this first step theoretical values of the roughness (Table 4) were adopted [36].
Figure 13 shows different steps in the procedure; in this case, the application
loaded a pre-processed .png image containing colour information derived by software and associates with each specific zone the corresponding roughness. The
limit of flooding was calculated according to the procedure described in the pre-
ceding section; flooding maximum value, about 210 m, is attained in correspondence of the widest inlet. The obtained values justify the accumulation of large
boulders in the first 100 m of the promontory; moreover maximum flooding is
recognisable in correspondence of inlets and at dune belt gap. Strong slowdown
occurs in correspondence of areas with higher presence of vegetation.

Table 4: Applying Chow's theory and considering the local morphology: Manning's numbers have been calculated empirically; the proposed table is improved by the field observation proposed by Tanaka *et al.* [21] and digital elaboration from Pignatelli *et al.* [26, 27].

Coastal types	Manning number (n)
Lagoon, fluvial plain	0.01–0.015
Mediterranean vegetation	0.016–0.025
Farm area	0.026–0.035
Discontinues dune belts (without vegetation)	0.036–0.040
Dune belts (altitude >3 m)	0.041–0.046
Rocky coasts (very karsificated)	0.047–0.052
Urban area discontinuous	0.053–0.058
Urban area (with buildings very concentrated)	0.059–0.064
Mangroves	0.065–0.069
Forests, Pinewood, etc.	>0.075

The second test performed the automatic recognition of surface types based on the different degree of colouring in the orthophoto and/or in the digital image supplied as input. However, the definition of boundaries between the different areas is very difficult due to the high number of classes and colours in the orthophoto. This does not allow us to clearly distinguish different types of surface. At this state of the art, we preferred to choose only three types of surfaces clearly identifiable in order to limit the error in the definition of the flooding area.

The model could be improved by including in the algorithm coefficients of roughness directly derived from TLS. By applying such methodology to the limited band next to the block, it is possible to obtain a realistic estimate of roughness coefficient, referred to the time when scanning was performed, and consequently an updated estimation of flooding area due to future tsunami(s).

The TLS points cloud allowed to obtain information concerning the Manning number only for the coastal areas described earlier. These were recognized and mapped using the ArcMap editor, and the resulting image was imported in the application of the model of flooding (Fig. 13).

At present, we are working to *(i)* improve the capacity of the system to connect the features of the image or the orthophoto to a Manning number directly derived by TLS surveys; *(ii)* match the orientation of the pixels to the direction of provenance of the simulated wave.

In the first test, the analysed image presented a certain level detail with respect to different types of soil use and of lithological types. However, in the second test, a greater detail of micro-topographic data only of the limited areas scanned by TLS has been obtained. In particular, the mean Manning numbers for the three different bands described earlier for the three different studied areas have been obtained. Both models indicate a limit of flooding no greater than 250 m. This value suggests that it may not be necessary to examine the entire area comprised

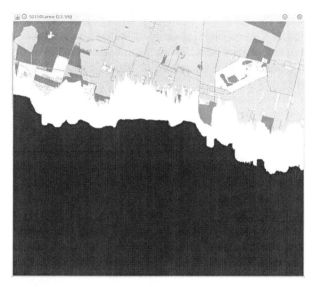

Figure 14: Estimated flooding due to the impact of a tsunami characterized by
$H_T = 8$ m.

in the orthophoto; it could be enough to restrict the survey to a strip not very extended inland but limited to a few hundred meters from the point in which the largest boulder has been detected. It is evident that the calculation of Manning number for the entire coastal area allows the construction of different flooding scenarios in response to different tsunamis (Fig. 14). Unfortunately, the fast evolution of the coastal area due to physical (mass movement, weathering, abrasion, sand deposition, growth of the vegetation) and anthropic processes produce Manning number change so that the availability of updated data is absolutely necessary in the implementation of the Integrated Coastal Zone Management plans and of first aid intervention plans.

Acknowledgements

This study was performed thanks to the Taranto Municipality that financially supported the project "Dinamica estrema ed erosione costiera lungo la costa ionica tarantina" managed by the II Facoltà di Scienze MM.FF & NN in Taranto, Università degli Studi "Aldo Moro", Bari (Sc. Resp.: Prof. G. Mastronuzzi), and thanks to the Italian Project RITMARE (Sc. Resp. Research Unit of the University of Bari: Prof. G. Mastronuzzi). We would like to express our gratitude to the Assessore Dott. Avv. Paolo Ciocia who promoted this study.

The paper is an Italian contribution to the project IGCP 588 – International Geological Correlation Programme "Preparing for coastal change. A detailed response process framework for coastal change at different times" by UNESCO – IUGS ((project Leaders: Dr. Adam D. Switzer, Earth Observatory of Singapore

(EOS), Nanyang Technological University, Dr. Craig Sloss, School of Natural resources Sciences, Queensland University of Technology, Australia, Dr. Benjamin Horton, Department of Earth and Environmental Sciences, University of Pennsylvania, Dr. Yongqiang Zong, Department of Earth Sciences, University of Hong Kong, China).

References

[1] Scheffers, A., Tsunami imprints on the Leeward Netherlands Antilles (Aruba, Curaçao and Bonaire) and their relation to other coastal problems. *Quaternary International*, **120(1)**, pp. 163–172, 2004.
[2] Mastronuzzi, G., Sansò, P., Bruckner, H., Pignatelli, C., Vott, A. Caputo, R., Coppola, D., Di Bucci, D., Fracassi, U., May, S.M, Milella, M. & Selleri, G, *Paleotsunami imprints along the coast of the central Mediterranean Sea.* 2nd International Tsunami Field Symposium. Ostuni (Puglia, Italy) – Lefkas (Ionian Islands, Greece), 21–27 September 2003, GI2S Coast – Gruppo Informale di Studi Costieri, Research Publication, 7, Digilabs s.r.l, Bari, 2008.
[3] Williams, D.M. & Hall, A.M, Cliff-top megaclast deposits of Ireland, a record of extreme waves in the North Atlantic—storms or tsunamis? *Marine Geology*, **206**, pp. 101–117, 2004.
[4] Goto, K, Chavanich, S.A, Imamura, F, Kunthasap, P, Matsui, T, Minoura, K, Sugawara, D. & Yanagisawa, H., Distribution, origin and transport process of boulders deposited by the 2004 Indian Ocean tsunami at Pakarang Cape, Thailand. *Sedimentary Geology*, **202**, pp. 821–837, 2007.
[5] Mastronuzzi, G., Pignatelli, C., Sansò, P. & Selleri, G., Boulder accumulations produced by the 20th February 1743 tsunami along the coast of southeastern Salento (Apulia region, Italy). *Marine Geology*, **242**, pp. 191–205, 2007.
[6] Goff, J., Weiss, R., Courtney, C. & Dominey-Howes, D., Testing the hypothesis for tsunami boulder deposition from suspension. *Marine Geology*, **277**, pp. 73–77, 2010.
[7] Barbano, M.S, Pirrotta, C. & Gerardi, F., Large boulders along the southeastern Ionian coast of Sicily: storm or tsunami deposits? *Marine Geology*, **275**, pp. 140–154, 2010.
[8] Switzer, A.D. & Burston, J.M, Competing mechanisms for boulder deposition on the southeast Australian coast. *Geomorphology*, **114**, 42e54, 2010.
[9] Mastronuzzi, G. & Pignatelli, C., The boulders berm of Punta Saguerra (Taranto, Italy): a morphological imprint of 4th April, 1836 Rossano Calabro tsunami? *Earth Planets Space*, **64**, pp. 1–14, 2010.
[10] Mastronuzzi, G., Brückner, H., De Martini, Regnauld, H., Tsunami: from the open sea to the coastal zone and beyond. *This volume*, 2012.
[11] Nott, J., Waves, coastal boulders and the importance of the pre-transport setting. *Earth Planetary Science Letters*, **210**, pp. 269–276, 2003.

[12] Noormets, R., Crook, K.A.W. & Felton, E.A, Sedimentology of rocky shore-lines: 3. Hydrodynamics of megaclast emplacement and transport on a shore platform, Oahu, Hawaii. *Sedimentary Geology*, **172**, pp. 41–65, 2004.

[13] Pignatelli, C. & Sansò, P. & Mastronuzzi, G., Evaluation of tsunami flooding using geomorphologic evidence. *Marine Geology*, **260**, pp. 6–18, 2009.

[14] Nandasena, N.A.K, Paris, R. & Tanaka, N., Reassessment of hydrodynamic equations: minimum flow velocity to initiate boulder transport by high energy events (storms, tsunamis). *Marine Geology*, **281**, pp. 70–84, 2011.

[15] Benner, R., Browne, T., Brückner, H., Kelletat, D. & Scheffers, A., Boulder transport by waves: progress in physical modeling. *Zeitschrift für Geomorphologie*, **54(3)**, pp. 127–146, 2010.

[16] Engel, M. & May, S.M, Bonaire's boulder fields revisited: evidence for Holocene tsunami impact on the Leeward Antilles. *Quaternary Science Review*, **54**, pp. 126–141, 2012.

[17] Hills, J.G. & Mader C.L, Tsunami produced by the impacts of the small asteroids. *Annals of the New York Academy of Sciences*, **822**, pp. 381–394, 1997.

[18] Bryant, E.A, *Tsunami: The Underratead Hazard*. Cambridge University Press: Cambridge, 2001.

[19] Manning, R., On the flow of water in open channels and pipes. *Transaction of the Institution of Civil Engineers* (Ireland), 1891.

[20] Chow, V.T, *Open-Channel Hydraulics*. McGraw-Hill: New York, 1973.

[21] Tanaka, N.Y, Sasaki, M.I.M, Mowjood, K.B, Jindasa, S.N. & Homchuen, S., Coastal Vegetation structures and their function in tsunami protection: experience of the recent Indian Ocean tsunami. *Landscape Ecology Engineering*, **3(1)**, pp. 33–45, 2007.

[22] Asal, F.F.F, *Airborne Remote Sensing for Landscape Modelling*. PhD thesis, The University of Nottingham, UK, 2003.

[23] Aberle, J., Dittrich, A. & Nestmann, F., *Description of Steep Stream Roughness with the Standard Deviations* S. Proc, XXVIII IAHR Biennial Congress, Graz, Austria, on CDROM, 1999.

[24] Smart, G.M, *An Improved Flow Resistance Formula*. River Flow 2004. Proceedings of the second International Conference on Fluvial Hydraulics, 23–25 June, Napoli, Italy, eds. M. Greco, A. Carravetta & R. Della Morte, Taylor & Francis, vol. 1, 2004.

[25] Smart, G. M., Duncan, M. J. & Walsh, J., Relatively rough flow resistance equations. *Journal of Hydraulic Engineering*, ASCE, **128(6)**, pp. 568–578, 2002.

[26] Pignatelli, C., Piscitelli, A., Damato, B. & Mastronuzzi, G., Estimation of the value of Manning's coefficient using Terrestrial Laser Scanner techniques for the assessment of extreme waves flooding. *Zeitschrift für Geomorphologie*, **54(3)**, pp. 317–336, 2010a.

[27] Pignatelli, C., Ferilli, S., Capolongo, D., Marsico, A., Milella, M., Pennetta, L., Piscitelli, A. & Mastronuzzi, G., Evidenze morfologiche, rilievo digitale ed applicazioni informatiche al fine della valutazione del limite di inondazione da tsunami. *Italian Journal of Remote Sensing*, **42(2)**, pp. 129–142, 2010b.

[28] Mastronuzzi, G. & Sansò, P., Boulders transport by catastrophic waves along the Ionian coast of Apulia (Southern Italy). *Marine Geology*, **170**, pp. 93–103, 2000.

[29] Mastronuzzi, G. & Sansò, P., Large boulder accumulations by extreme waves along the Adriatic coast of southern Apulia (Italy). *Quaternary International*, **120**, pp. 173–184, 2004.

[30] Mastronuzzi, G. & Sansò, P. (eds), *Quaternary Coastal Morphology and Sea Level Changes.* Puglia 2003, Final Conference. Project IGCP 437 UNESCO - IUGS, Otranto/Taranto - Puglia (Italy) 22–28 September 2003, GI2S Coast Coast – Gruppo Informale di Studi Costieri, Research Publication, 5, Brizio srl – Taranto, 2003.

[31] Minelli, A. (ed), La Macchia mediterranea. Formazioni sempreverdi costiere. *Quaderni Habitat*, n.6, Ministero dell'Ambiente e della Tutela del Territorio e del Mare, Museo Friulano di Storia Naturale, Comune di Udine, 2002.

[32] Laborel, J. & Laborel-Deguen, F., Biological indicators of relative sea-level variations and of co-seismic displacements in the Mediteranean region. *Journal of Coastal Research*, **10(2)**, pp. 395–415, 1994.

[33] Marsico, A., Pignatelli, C., Piscitelli, A., Mastronuzzi, G. & Pennetta, L., *Ricostruzione digitale di blocchi accumulati da eventi estremi in Italia meridionale.* Atti 13a Conferenza Nazionale ASITA, 1–4 dicembre 2009, pp. 1377–1385, 2009.

[34] Paris, R., Fournier, J., Poizot, E., Etienne, S., Morin, J., Lavigne, F. & Wassmer, P., Boulder and fine sediment transport and deposition by the 2004 tsunami in Lhok Nga (western Banda Aceh, Sumatra, Indonesia): a coupled offshore—onshore model. *Marine Geology*, **268**, pp. 43–54, 2010.

[35] Helley, E.J., *Field Measurement of the Initiation of Large Bed Particle Motion in Blue Creek near Klamath*, California. U.S. Geological Survey Professional Paper 562-G, 1969.

[36] Arcement, G., Schneider, V., *Guide for selecting Manning's roughness coefficients for natural channels and flood plains.* U.S. Geological Survey, Water Supply Paper 2339, 1989.

CHAPTER 4

Tsunami early warning coordination centres

J. Santos-Reyes[1] & A.N. Beard[2]
[1]SARACS Research Group, SEPI-ESIME, Instituto Politecnico Nacional, Mexico
[2]Civil Engineering Section, Heriot-Watt University, Edinburgh, United Kingdom

Abstract

Following the tsunami disaster in 2004, the General Secretary of the United Nations (UN) Kofi Annan called for a 'global early warning system' for all hazards and for all communities. He also requested the International Strategy for Disaster Reduction and its UN partners to conduct a global survey of capacities, gaps and opportunities in relation to 'early warning systems'. The produced report, 'Global Survey of Early Warning Systems', concluded that there are many gaps and shortcomings and that much progress has been made on early warning systems and great capabilities are available around the world. However, it may be argued that an 'early warning system' (EWS) may not be enough to prevent fatalities due to tsunami. That is, an EWS should be seen as part of a 'total disaster management system'. Moreover, it may be argued that an EWS may work very well when assessed individually but it is less clear whether it will contribute to accomplish the purpose of a 'total disaster management system' when assessed as a 'whole', that is, to prevent fatalities. There is a need for a systemic approach to 'tsunami early warning systems'. The chapter presents a model for a 'tsunami early warning system'.
Keywords: *coordination centres, disaster, early warning system, risk, SDMS model, systemic, tsunami*

1 Introduction

The United Nations International Strategy for Disaster Reduction (UN/ISDR) has defined a 'disaster' as 'a serious disruption of the functioning of a community or a society causing widespread human, material, economic or environmental losses that exceeds the ability of the affected community or society to cope using its own resources' [1]. A 'natural disaster', on the other hand, is defined as a result of a 'serious disruption triggered by a natural hazard (e.g. earthquakes, hurricanes, floods, windstorms, landslides, volcanic eruptions and wildfires) causing human, material, economic or environmental losses that exceed the ability of those affected to cope' [1, 2]. Some statistics on disasters published in the literature show that between 1995 and 2004 there were about 6000 disasters accounting for about 900,000 people dead, US$738 billion material losses and 2500 million people affected [2–6].

Recent tsunamis (i.e. a series of travelling waves of extremely long length and period, usually generated by earthquakes occurring below or near the ocean floor, volcanic eruptions, submarine landslides, coastal rock falls or large meteorite impacting the ocean [7].) have highlighted the devastating consequences of 'natural disasters'. On 26 December, 2004, one of the biggest earthquake in 40 years occurred between the Australian and Eurasian plates in the Indian Ocean. The quake triggered a tsunami that spread thousands of kilometres over several hours. It is believed that several waves of that tsunami came at the intervals of 5 and 40 min [8, 9]. For instance, in Kalutara (a tourist resort in Sri Lanka) the water reached at least 1 km inland, causing widespread destruction and death. The disaster left at least 165,000 people dead, more than half a million more were injured and up to 5 million others in need of basic services and at risk of deadly epidemics in a dozen Indian Ocean countries [8, 9].

More recently, on 11 March, 2011, an earthquake and a tsunami struck Japan that was followed by a nuclear crisis; it is believed that the magnitude of the Tohoku earthquake was estimated to be 9.0 on the Richter scale which places it as the fourth largest in the world since 1900 and the largest in Japan since modern instrumental recordings began 130 years ago [10]. Some of the losses of the disaster are thought to be the following: at least 15,703 people killed, 4647 missing, 5314 injured, 130,927 displaced and at least 332,395 buildings, 2126 roads, 56 bridges and 26 railways destroyed or damaged by the earthquake and tsunami along the entire east coast of Honshu from Chiba to Aomori [10].

Following the tsunami disaster in 2004, the General Secretary of the United Nations (UN), at the time, Kofi Annan, called for a 'global early warning system' for all hazards and for all communities [11]. He also requested the ISDR and its UN partners to conduct a global survey of capacities, gaps and opportunities in relation to 'early warning systems' (EWSs). The produced report, 'Global Survey of Early Warning Systems' [12], concluded that there are many gaps and shortcomings and that much progress has been made on EWSs and great capabilities are available around the world. According to the UN/ISDR, 'early warning' is defined as 'the provision of timely and effective information, through identified institutions, that allows individuals exposed to a hazard to take action to avoid or reduce their risk and prepare for effective response' [12]. On the other hand, 'early warning systems' include a chain of concerns, namely understanding and mapping the hazard, monitoring and forecasting impending events, processing and disseminating understandable warnings to political authorities and the population and undertaking appropriate and timely actions in response to the warnings [1, 2]. According to the UNISDR, 'effective early warning systems' have to integrate four elements: *(i)* the knowledge of the risks; *(ii)* technical monitoring and warning service; *(iii)* dissemination and communication of meaningful warnings to those at risk; *(iv)* public awareness and preparedness to react to warnings [6, 12].

As stated earlier, a number of studies have been reported in the literature on different aspects of the four elements of an 'effective early warning system', for example, studies on the implementation of tsunami EWS [13–15], awareness building, physical mitigation measures and hazard and risk mappings [16–31].

In this chapter, a model for a tsunami 'early warning coordination centre' is put forward. The subsequent sections will give an account of the ongoing research on 'early warning coordination centres' from a systemic point of view.

2 A systemic disaster management system model

A systemic disaster management system (SDMS) model has been constructed by adopting a systemic approach; the model is intended to maintain disaster risk within an acceptable range in an organization's operations. The model is proposed as a sufficient structure for an effective disaster management system. It has a fundamentally preventive potentiality in that if all the subsystems and connections are present and working effectively the probability of a failure should be less than otherwise. Table 1 summarises the structural organization of the SDMS model. See [32–36] for details of the origin and development of the model and a full account of the fundamental characteristics of the model. A brief description of the structural organization of the model will be given in the subsequent sections.

2.1 The basic structural organization of the model

Figure 1 shows the structural organization of the model, that is, Systems 1–5. Overall, the structure of the organization of the model shown in Fig. 1 can be divided

Table 1: Structural organization of a SDMS model. (©JR Santos-Reyes & AN Beard, 2012).

A structural organization that consists of a 'basic unit' in which it is necessary to achieve five functions associated with Systems 1–5. (See Fig. 1).
(a) System 1: disaster-policy implementation
(b) System 2: 'total early warning coordination centre' ('TEWCC')
(c) System 2*: 'local early warning coordination centre' ('LEWC')
(d) System 3: disaster functional
(e) System 3*: disaster audit
(f) System 4: disaster development
(g) System 4*: disaster confidential reporting system
(h) System 5: disaster policy

Note: whenever a line appears in Fig. 1 representing the SDMS model, it represents a channel of communication.

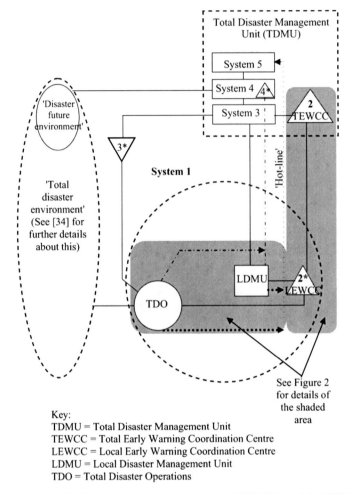

Figure 1. A systemic disaster management system (SDMS) model. (©JR Santos-Reyes & AN Beard, 2012).

into two parts. One part consists of the collection of subsystems that constitute System 1 (i.e. System 1 can be decomposed into several subsystems; see Section 3 for further details). The second part consists of the collection of the subsystems 2–5 intended to look after the collection the subsystems that constitute System 1, so that they cohere in that totality that is called here a 'disaster management system-in-focus' (DMS-in-focus), that is, the ones shown in Figs. 1–4. (In fact, in the context of the model, there could be several 'DMS-in-focuses' nested vertically when modelling DMS for a particular country or region). A brief account of each of the subsystems is given in the following. Referring to Fig. 1:

(a) System 1: disaster policy implementation, LDMU (local disaster management unit) implements safety policies in TDO (total disaster operations) in relation

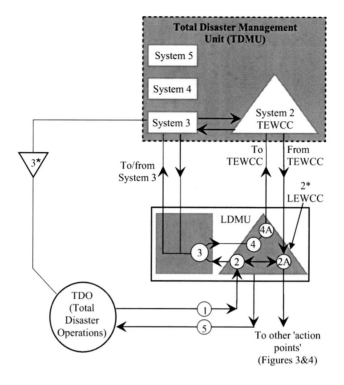

Key:
TDMU = Total Disaster Management Unit
TEWCC = Total Early Warning Coordination Centre
LEWCC = Local Early Warning Coordination Centre
LDMU = Local Disaster Management Unit
TDO = Total Disaster Operations

Figure 2. System 2: an EWCC. (©JR Santos-Reyes & AN Beard, 2012).

to the disaster risk. (It should be emphasised that 'TDO' refers to all the activities government/general public do in their daily lives; moreover, it is here where disaster risk is created, for example, general public/communities unprepared for an emergency, lack of funds for the implementation of 'EWSs', critical infrastructures not being protected against natural hazards, inadequate/inexistent infrastructures to protect civilians/communities against natural hazards, etc.). System 1 can be decomposed into several operations on the basis of geography, for example, 'disaster operations' at an international, national, subnational levels (see later sections for details about this).

(b) System 2: TEWCC (Total Early Warning Coordination Centre) coordinates all the activities of the 'disaster operations' that form part of System 1 (Fig. 1) and in relation to the 'total environment'. Moreover, it also coordinates other 'local early warning coordination centres' (LEWCCs). System 2 along with System 1 implements the safety plans received from System 3.

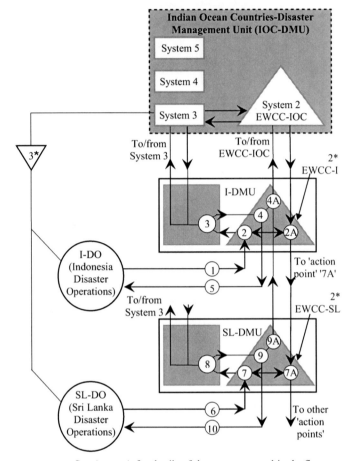

See Annex-A for details of the acronyms used in the figure.

Figure 3. EWCC-Two Indian Ocean countries are shown. (©JR Santos-Reyes & AN Beard, 2012).

(c) System 2*: LEWCC is part of System 2, and is responsible for communicating advance warnings to other 'early warning coordination centres' and to key decision makers in order to take appropriate actions prior to the occurrence of a major natural hazard event.

(d) System 3: disaster functional is directly responsible for maintaining disaster risk within an acceptable range, whatever that might be, in System 1 operations on a daily basis. It ensures that System 1 implements the organization's safety policy.

(e) System 3*: disaster audit, is part of System 3 and its function is to conduct audits sporadically into the operations of System 1. System 3* intervenes in the operations of System 1 according to the safety plans received from System 3.

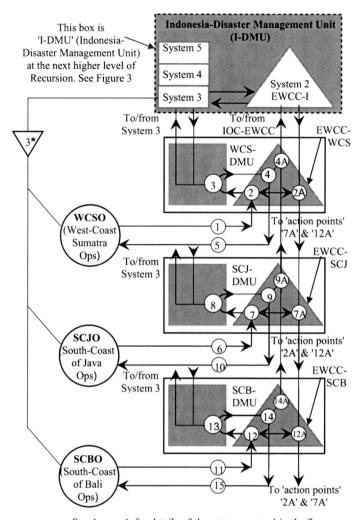

Figure 4. EWCC-The case of Indonesia. (©JR Santos-Reyes & AN Beard, 2012).

(f) System 4: disaster development is generally concerned with the 'total environment' and its function is to conduct research and development (R&D) for the
continual adaptation of the organization. By considering strengths, weak-
nesses, threats and opportunities, System 4 can suggest changes to the organization's safety policies. (e.g. EWS and the impacts of climate change).

(g) System 4*: disaster confidential reporting system is part of System 4 and it is
concerned with confidential reports or causes of concern from any person of
the public about any aspects, some of which may require the direct intervention
of System 5.

(h) System 5: disaster policy is responsible for deliberating safety policies and for making strategic decisions. System 5 also monitors the activities of System 4 and System 3.
(i) 'Hot-line': Fig. 1 shows a dashed line directly from System 1 to System 5, representing a direct communication or 'hot-line' for use in exceptional circumstances, for example, during an emergency.

The subsequent sections will present a description of System 2, early warning coordination centre, only. For a full account of the model and some of its applications in relation to disaster management see [32, 36].

2.2 System 2: early warning coordination centre

The function of System 2 is to coordinate the activities of the operations of System 1. To achieve the plans of System 3 and the needs of System 1, System 2 gathers and manages the safety information of System 1's operations. In a relatively well-coordinated system, the information flows might be according to the arrangement shown in Fig. 2. In general, the arrangement indicates that if a deviation occurs from the accepted criteria (e.g. a tsunami), then the functions of the 'LEWCC' within System 1 are the following:

Firstly, to detect any deviation from the accepted criteria (e.g. a tsunami) (see action point '2' in Fig. 2). Secondly, to issue the warning simultaneously to

(a) 'LDMU' that in turn implements the pre-planned 'measures' in the operations (e.g. evacuation, search and rescue, emergency medical services); see action points 3, 4 and 5 in Fig. 2.
(b) other 'LEWCCs' through action point '2A' (this is not shown in Fig. 2 but see Figs 3 and 4 where other 'action points' are shown). Similarly, these coordination centres have to assess consequences and implement 'measures' within their operations and to make reports quickly to System 2 (TEWCC); see Fig. 2.
(c) System 2 (TEWCC) through action point '4A'. By receiving the warning it takes fast corrective action, either through the channels of communication that connects the 'LEWCC' or via System 3 and this is shown in Fig. 2. (Some of the functions of the 'TEWCC' are the collection and compilation of information from the affected areas, supply of information to System 3).

The following section presents an example of the application of the coordination arrangement described earlier. The case of Indonesia will be used to illustrate this feature of the model.

3 Modelling EWCC for the case of an Indian Ocean Country

It is believed the Indian Ocean tsunami on 26 December, 2004, began at 7:58 am, triggered by one of the most powerful earthquake measuring 9.0 on the Richter scale. The earthquake centred off the coast of Sumatra, Indonesia, it struck 30 km below the sea level, and the resulting tsunami travelled at speeds up to 800 km/h.

The tsunami struck the coast of Aceh within minutes, Sri Lanka within 3 h. Indonesia was one of the hardest hit by the tsunami.

Figures 3 and 4 show the 'EWCCs' for the case of Indonesia. It also can be seen in Fig. 3 that only two Indian Ocean countries are shown, that is, 'Indonesia Disaster Operations' (IDO) and 'Sri Lanka-Disaster Operations' (SL-DO). However, it is possible, in principle, to model a 'disaster management system' for all the Indian Ocean countries (i.e. India, Indonesia, Maldives, Sri Lanka, Thailand, etc.) with their associated 'EWCCs'. One of the key concepts within the SDMS model is concerned with the principle of 'recursion', that is, a 'disaster management system' (DMS) is embedded within another DMS and that the structural organization (i.e. Systems 1–5) is replicated at every level of recursion. This means that there could be several 'DMSs' interconnected 'vertically' at national, regional or at community levels and for any country.

As given earlier, Fig. 3 may be regarded as the top level of recursion of our interest, that is, 'Indonesia-Disaster Operations' (IDO). By moving down one level below this, three subsystems have been identified, that is, 'West Coast of Sumatra Operations' (WCSO), South Coast of Java Operations (SCJO) and South Coast of Bali Operations (SCBO) as shown in Fig. 4. It should be emphasised that 'IDO' has been decomposed into the three mentioned subsystems; however, other regions or areas within the country may be considered for a full application of the model; this consideration has been made in order to illustrate the features of the model.

Tables 2 and 3 present a description of the arrangement shown in Fig. 4. It also has been assumed that a deviation from the acceptable criteria occurred in the 'WCSO, that is, 'action point' '2' in Fig. 4. However, a tsunami can be detected in either action point '7' or '12'.

It has been argued that had a tsunami early warning system (EWS) been operational in the Indian Ocean, like the international tsunami warning system that covers the Pacific Ocean, the human toll might only have been a fraction of what it was [4]. However, the most recent tsunami and earthquake of 11 March, 2011, that struck Japan has demonstrated that this is not necessarily the case. That is, an EWS may work very well when assessed individually but it is less clear whether it will contribute to saving lives when the 'total disaster management system' is assessed as a 'whole'. It may be argued that Japan is equipped with the most advanced 'tsunami warning system' in the world. However, the aftermath of the disaster with the death toll about 20,000 has raised many questions, for example, Why did some people not evacuate and others did? Did they receive the tsunami warning? How can a tsunami warning be understandable and effective?

It has been argued here and elsewhere [33–35] that an EWS should be seen as part of a 'total disaster management system'. For example, a regional EWS may only work if it is well co-ordinated with the local warning and emergency response systems that ensure that the warning is received, communicated and acted upon by the potentially affected communities. It also may be argued that without these local measures being in place, a regional EWS will have little impact in saving lives. Researchers argued that unless people are warned in remote areas, the technology is useless, for example, McGuire (cited in [37]) argues that 'I have no

Table 2: 'Action points'-Fig. 3. (©JR Santos-Reyes & AN Beard, 2012).

Action point	Description
①	Flow of data related to any particular sensor and monitoring system (e.g. those related to earthquake/tsunami: ocean bottom pressure sensors, buoys, tide gauges, etc. [7, 13, 15–17, 26]). The data communications may be done via wire line, wireless, satellite, etc.
②	Analysis of the data being received. If any deviation from the pre-planned acceptable criteria occurs (e.g. a tsunami) then it issues the tsunami warning to action points '2A' and '3' as shown in Fig. 4. (Assuming that the tsunami has been detected at the 'West Coast of Sumatra Operations' (WCSO)).
③	Action points '3' and '4', within the 'WCSO', plan and take 'measures' to respond to the tsunami warning. Action point '3' also issues the warning to System 3 (Fig. 4).
④	Planning and taking effective 'measures' in order to respond to the tsunami warning and these should be the result of a tsunami risk assessment, for example, the generation of hazard, exposure, response and risk maps. These maps may help to provide the overall risk for a particular country, region, area, etc. Areas with 'high risk' can be identified and can be used, for example, to better plan the mitigation 'measures'. [13–15].
⑤	(a) The tsunami warning is issued. The public at risk may be informed by the use of a variety of existing communication technologies (e.g. public address systems, radio, TV, etc. [36]). However, the communication of the warnings should be effective so that the public should be able to clearly understand what to do before/during/after, for example, a tsunami. (b) Implementation of pre-planned 'measures' to evacuate safely and prevent fatalities due to a tsunami. As mentioned earlier, the 'measures' should consider, for example, the 'Estimated time of arrival' (ETA) of a tsunami in the evacuation plans. (ETA has been defined as the time needed for the tsunami wave to propagate from the earthquake source location to the coast [13, 26]).
	The 'measures' should also consider explicitly the people's response to such warnings, for example, the time taken by people at risk from receiving the warning and their decision to react and to evacuate, that is, the 'evacuation time' (time that people need for evacuation to reach safe areas) [13, 26].

doubt that the technical element of the warning system will work very well',... 'But there has to be an effective and efficient communications cascade from the warning centre to the fisherman on the beach and his family and the bar owners'. Similarly, McFadden (cited in [38]) states that 'There's no point in spending all the money on a fancy monitoring and a fancy analysis system unless we can make sure the infrastructure for the broadcast system is there',... 'That's going to require a lot of work. If it's a tsunami, you've got to get it down to the last Joe on the beach. This is the stuff that is really very hard'.

Table 3: The coordination function of the 'EWCCs'. (©JR Santos-Reyes & AN Beard, 2012).

Action point	Description
(2A)	Once a tsunami has been detected, then action point '2' transmits the warning to action point '2A' that in turn performs the following functions: (a) communicates the tsunami warning to other 'early warning coordination centres', e.g. 'EWCC-SCJ' (Early Warning Coordination Centre-South Coast of Java) and 'EWCC-SCB' (Early Warning Coordination Centre-South Coast of Bali) through the action points '7A' and '12A', respectively, as shown in Fig. 4.
(4A)	Issues the warning and the 'measures' taken as a response to the tsunami warning to the 'EWCC-I' (System 2 in Fig. 4) and by receiving all this information; the 'EWCC-I' enables to take a 'higher' order view of the total consequences. 'EWCC-I' will also make reports to System 3. Moreover, once the 'EWCC-I', at this level of recursion, receives the tsunami warning it will communicate about it to 'early warning coordination centres' at the next higher level of recursion, that is (a) other EWCCs of the Indian Ocean Countries, for example, 'EWCC-SL' (Early Warning Coordination Centre-Sri Lanka) as shown in Fig. 3; (b) to 'EWCC-IOC' (Early Warning Coordination Centre-Indian Ocean Countries) (Fig. 3) that in turn will communicate the tsunami warning to say a 'global early warning system'.

4 Conclusions and future work

A systemic disaster management system (SDMS) model has been proposed to manage disaster risk effectively [32, 36]. The Chapter has presented one of the features of the model, that is, an 'Early Warning Coordination Centre' (EWCC) that is associated with one of the functions of the model, that is, System 2 (a subsystem that constitute the 'basic unit' of highly interacting subsystems 1–5 of the structural organization of the model). To illustrate the communication channels amongst 'EWCCs', the case of Indonesia has been used to illustrate this. Research is being conducted on a number of issues, for example, the developed model is being applied to modelling, a 'global early warning' system; moreover, research on effective communication of warnings is also being undertaken. Overall, it may be argued that the approach presented here may help us to gain a better understanding of 'early warnings', in general, and it is also hoped that this approach will help to provide '...an effective and efficient communications cascade from the warning centre to the fisherman on the beach & his family and the bar owners' (cited in [37]).

Acknowledgements

This project was funded by SIP-IPN under the following grant: SIP-20120295.

Annexure A

IOC-DMU   Indian Ocean Countries-Disaster Management Unit
I-DO   Indonesia-Disaster Operations
I-DMU   Indonesia-Disaster Management Unit
SL-DO   Sri Lanka-Disaster Operations
SL-DMU   Sri Lanka-Disaster Management Unit
EWCC-IOC   Early Warning Coordination Centres-Indian Ocean Countries
EWCC-I   Early Warning Coordination Centre-Indonesia
EWCC-SL   Early Warning Coordination Centre-Sri Lanka
WCSO   West Coast Sumatra Operations
WCS-DMU   West Coast Sumatra-Disaster Management Unit
SCJO   South Coast of Java Operations
SCJ-DMU   South Coast of Java-Disaster Management Unit
SCBO   South Coast of Bali Operations
SCB-DMU   South Coast of Bali-Disaster Management Unit
EWCC-WCS   Early Warning Coordination Centre-West Coast of Sumatra
EWCC-SCJ   Early Warning Coordination Centre-South Coast of Java
EWCC-SCB   Early Warning Coordination Centre-South Coast of Bali

References

[1] UN/ISDR, *Terminology: basic terms of disaster risk reduction.* available at http://www.unisdr.org/eng/library/lib-terminology-eng%20home.htm, International Strategy for Disaster Reduction secretariat, Geneva. 2004.

[2] UN/ISDR, *Reducing disaster risk - a challenge for development.* United Nations Development Programme (UNDP), 2004, Online. www.undp.org/bcpr.

[3] IFRC, *World disasters report 2005.* (Disasters data prepared by the Centre for Research on the Epidemiology of Disasters from the EM-DAT database.) International Federation of Red Cross and Red Crescent Societies, Geneva. 2005.

[4] UN/ISDR, *Disaster statistics 1994–2004.* (Prepared in collaboration with the Centre for Research on the Epidemiology of Disasters from the EM-DAT database.) available at http://www.unisdr.org/disaster-statistics/introduction. htm. International Strategy for Disaster Reduction Secretariat, Geneva. 2005.

[5] CRED, *Data from EM-DAT, the OFDA/CRED International Disaster Database*, available at www.em-dat.net, Centre for Research on the Epidemiology of Disasters (CRED), Universite´Catholique de Louvain, Brussels, Belgium. (OFDA is the US Office of Foreign Disaster Assistance.) 2005.

[6] Bashir, R., Global early warning systems for natural hazards: systematic and people centred. *Philosophical Transactions of the Royal Society* A **364**, pp. 2167–2182, 2006.

[7] UNESCO, *Tsunami glossary.* IOC Information document No. 1221. Paris, UNESCO, 2006. available at http://ioc3.unesco.org/itic/files/tsunami_glossary_en_small.pdf (accessed 10 February 2012.)

[8] BBC, Tsunami disaster. Online. available at http://news.bbc.co.uk/go/pr/fr/-/1/hi/world/asia-pacific/4136289.stm

[9]   UNDP, *Survivors of the tsunami: One year later*. United Nations Develop-
      ment Programme (UNDP), 2005, Online. available at www.undp.org/bcpr.
[10] USGS (United States Geological Survey), Magnitude 9.0-Near the east coast
      of Honshu, Japan. available at http://earthquake.usgs.gov/earthquakes/recen-
      teqsww/Quakes/usc0001xgp.php (accessed 10 February 2012.)
[11] Annan, K., In the Secretary-General's report "In larger Freedom". Report
      A/59/2005, paragraph 66, 2005.
[12] United Nations International Strategy for Disaster Reduction (UN/ISDR),
      2006, Global survey of early warning systems. United Nations International
      Strategy for Disaster Reduction (UN/ISDR), Geneva.
[13] Strunz, G., Post, J., Zosseder, K., Wegscheider, S., Mück, M., Riedlinger,
      T., Mehl, H., Dech, S., Birkmann, J., Gebert, N., Harjono, H., Anwar, H.Z.,
      Sumaryono, Khomarudin, R.M. & Muhari, A., Tsunami risk assessment in
      Indonesia. *Nat. Hazards Earth Syst. Sci.*, **11**, pp. 67–82, 2011. www.nat-
      hazards-earth-syst-sci.net/11/67/2011/doi:10.5194/nhess-11-67-2011. 2011.
[14] Rudloff, A., Lauterjung, J., Münch, U. & Tinti, S., Preface "The GITEWS
      Project (German–Indonesian Tsunami Early Warning System)". *Natural
      Hazards and Earth Systems Sciences* **9**, pp. 1381–1382, 2009. doi:10.5194/
      nhess-9-1381-2009.
[15] Behrens, J., Androsov, A., Babeyko, A.Y., Harig, S., Klaschka, F. & Mentrup,
      L., A new multi-sensor approach to simulation assisted tsunami early warn-
      ing. *Natural Hazards and Earth Systems Sciences* **10**, pp. 1085–1100, 2010.
      doi:10.5194/nhess-10-1085-2010.
[16] Lauterjung, J., Münch, U. & Rudloff, A., The challenge of installing a tsu-
      nami early warning system in the vicinity of the Sunda Arc, Indonesia. *Nat-
      ural Hazards Earth Systems Science* **10**, pp. 641–646, 2010. doi:10.5194/
      nhess-10-641-2010.
[17] Review of tsunami hazard and risk in New Zealand. In: Berryman, K., et al.
      (Ed.), *Geological and Nuclear Sciences* (GNS) (report 2005/104. p.140). 2005.
[18] Burbidge, D. & Cummins, P., Assessing the threat to Western Australia from
      tsunami generated by earthquakes along the Sunda Arc. *Natural Hazards* **43**,
      pp. 319–331, 2007. doi:10.1007/s11069-007-9116-3.
[19] Tinti, S. & Armigliato, A., The use of scenarios to evaluate the tsunami
      impact in southern Italy. *Marine Geology* **199(3–4)**, pp. 221–243, 2003.
[20] Roemer, H., Kaiser, G., Sterr, H. & Ludwig, R., Using remote sensing to
      assess tsunami-induced impacts on coastal forest ecosystems at the Anda-
      man Sea coast of Thailand. *Natural Hazards and Earth Systems Sciences* **10**,
      pp. 729–745, 2010. doi:10.5194/nhess-10-729-2010.
[21] Brune, S., Babeyko, A.Y., Ladage, S. & Sobolev, S.V., Landslide tsunami
      hazard in the Indonesian Sunda Arc. *Natural Hazards and Earth System Sci-
      ences* **10**, pp. 589–604, 2010. doi:10.5194/nhess-10-589-2010.
[22] Lorito, S., Tiberti, M.M., Basili, R., Piatanesi, A. & Valensise, G., Earthquake-
      generated tsunamis in the Mediterranean Sea: scenarios of potential threats
      to Southern Italy. *Journal of Geophysical Research* **113(B1)**, pp. 1–14. 2008.
[23] Okal, E. & Synloakis, C.E., Far-field tsunami hazard from mega-thrust
      earthquakes in the Indian Ocean. *Geophysical Journal International* **172**,
      pp. 995–1015, 2008.

[24] Sengara, I.W., Latief, H. & Kusuma, S.B., Probabilistic seismic and tsunami hazard analysis for design criteria and disaster mitigation in rehabilitation and reconstruction of a coastal area in city of Banda Aceh. eds Liu, Deng, Chu, *Geotechnical Engineering for Disaster Mitigation and Rehabilitation.* Springer Verlag. 2008.

[25] Parsons, T. & Geist, E., Tsunami probability in the Caribbean Region. *Pure and Applied Geophysics* **165**, pp. 2089–2116, 2009.

[26] Post, J., Wegscheider, S., Mück, M., Zosseder, K., Kiefl, R., Steinmetz, T. & Strunz, G., Assessment of human immediate response capability related to tsunami threats in Indonesia at a sub-national scale. *Natural Hazards and Earth Systems Sciences* **9**, pp. 1075–1086, 2009.

[27] Power, W., Downes, G., Stirling, M., Estimation of tsunami hazard in New Zealand due to South American Earthquakes. *Pure and Applied Geophysics* **164**, pp. 547–564, 2007.

[28] Gayer, G., Leschka, S., Nöhren, I., Larsen, O. & Günther, H., Tsunami inundation modelling based on detailed roughness maps of densely populated areas. *Natural Hazards Earth and Systems Sciences* **10**, pp. 1679–1687, 2010. doi:10.5194/nhess-10-1679-2010.

[29] Okal, E.A., Borrero, J.C. & Synolakis, C.E., Evaluation of tsunami risk from regional earthquakes at Pisco, Peru. *Bulletin of the Seismological Society of America* **96(5)**, pp. 1634–1648, 2006.

[30] Geist, E. & Parsons, T., Probabilistic analysis of tsunami hazards. *Natural Hazards* **37**, pp. 277–314, 2006.

[31] Annaka, T., Satake, K., Sakakiyama, T., Yanagisawa, K. & Shuto, N., Logic-tree approach for probabilistic tsunami hazard analysis and its applications to the Japanese coasts. *Pure and Applied Geophysics* **164**, pp. 577–592, 2007.

[32] Santos-Reyes, J., & Beard, A.N., A systemic approach to fire safety management, *Fire Safety Journal*, **36**, pp. 359–390, 2001.

[33] Santos-Reyes, J., Early warning coordination centres: a systemic view, *Proceedings of Engineering Nature-2007- First International Conference on the Art of Resisting Extreme Natural Forces*, 11–13 July, 2007, Sussex, England, UK, ISBN: 978-1-84564-086-6.

[34] Jaime Santos-Reyes & Alan N Beard, A systemic approach to managing natural disasters- Book Chapter. eds Asimakopoulou & Bessis. *Adavanced ICTs for Disaster Management and Threat Detection*, IGI-Global, USA. 2010.

[35] Santos-Reyes, J. & Beard, A.N.,. Learning from Tabasco's floods by applying a SDMS model, *Human and Ecological Risk Assessment.* **17(3)**, pp. 646–677, 2011.ISSN: 1549-7860.

[36] Santos-Reyes, J., & Beard, A.N., Information communication technology and a systemic disaster management system model. *International Journal of Distributed Systems and Technologies (IJDST)*, **2(1)**, pp. 29–42, 2011.

[37] Kettlewell, J., Early warning technology – is it enough? Online. available at http://news.bbc.co.uk/go/pr/fr/-/2/hi/science/nature/4149201.stm. 2005.

[38] Kettlewell, J., Tsunami alert technology – the iron link. Online. available at http://news.bbc.co.uk/go/pr/fr/-/2/hi/science/nature/4373333.stm 2005.

CHAPTER 5

RC buildings performance under the 2011 great East Japan Tsunami

C. Cuadra
Department of Architectural and Environment Systems, Akita Prefectural University, Japan

Abstract

The Great East Japan Earthquake on 11 March, 2011 is the most powerful known earthquake that has hit Japan with a magnitude 9.0 and with epicentre located at 129 km of Sendai city (off the coast). The earthquake triggered a destructive tsunami with run-up height of up to 40 m that mainly affect cities located on the Pacific Ocean coast of the Tohoku region (north-east region of Japan). Reinforced concrete buildings in general resist the tsunami without collapse; however, the non-structural elements such as panels and ceilings were severely damaged. In this report, the characteristics of the damages and behaviour of RC buildings during the tsunami action are discussed based on the field damage survey in selected cities located on the coast of the affected zone. The analysis made us understand the behaviour of the kind of buildings under tsunami attack, and has also permitted us to establish recommendations for their use to take refuge from tsunami in places where natural topography makes impossible to reach hilltops or other safer places.
Keywords: East Japan Earthquake, RC buildings, seismic damage, tsunami

1 Introduction

An earthquake with a magnitude of Mw 9.0 struck the north-east part of Japan (Tohoku region), on 11 March, 2011, at 14:46 local time. This earthquake is the most powerful known earthquake that has hit Japan with its epicentre located at 129 km of Sendai city of north-east region of Japan. The earthquake triggered a destructive tsunami with run up height of up to 40 m. The tsunami affects cities mainly located on the Pacific Ocean coast of Iwate, Miyagi and Fukushima prefectures in the Tohoku region, and also Ibaraki prefecture in the Kanto region.

Wooden structures were destroyed by the tsunami action when the water depth reaches or covers at least the first floor of the building. These wooden structures were the most vulnerable constructions that were washed up by tsunami. Steel frame structures and steel trusses that are used mainly for industrial constructions suffer heavy damages of walls, ceilings, finishing panels and non-structural elements. In some cases, the failure of these non-structural components produces the failure of structural elements and even the collapse of the structure. Reinforced concrete (RC) buildings in general did resist the tsunami without collapse; however, the non-structural elements such as panels and ceilings were severely damaged. However, in some cases low-rise RC buildings were tilted by the tsunami action. In this chapter, the characteristics of the damages and behaviour of RC buildings during the tsunami action is discussed based on the field survey of the damages in selected cities located on the coast of the affected zone. The analysis made us understand the behaviour of the kind of buildings under tsunami attack and has also permitted us to establish recommendations for their use to take refuge from tsunami in places where natural topography makes impossible to reach hilltops or other safer places.

2 Characteristics of the earthquake and tsunami

The Great East Japan Earthquake that occurred on 11 March, 11 2011 (at 14:46) was an inter-plate earthquake that occurred on the boundary between the Pacific Ocean plate and the Continental plate (called American plate). This earthquake is also known as the 2011 off the Pacific Coast of Tohoku Earthquake or the 2011 Tohoku-Pacific Earthquake. The magnitude of the earthquake was reported as being Mw 9.0, which is the highest magnitude ever recorded in Japan.

2.1 Tsunami source

The Japanese Meteorological Agency (JMA) has reported an analysis of the tsunami source and its generation mechanism, based on the observed data [1]. The result of this analysis can be observed in Fig. 1. In total, data of 19 observation stations were used for the analysis. The observation points include the coast from Hokkaido (north of Japan) to Kanto region. From the arrival time observed in each stations and by means of an inverse analysis the tsunami source is estimated. As can be observed in Fig. 1, the source ranges from off the coast of Iwate prefecture to off the coast of Ibaraki prefecture that represents about 500 km of length and also the width of the source is estimated to be 200 km.

The validity of the estimation of the tsunami source area is verified by comparing it with the distribution of the aftershocks. The distribution of these aftershocks (with magnitude larger than 5), According to the Japanese Meteorological Agency, is shown in Fig. 2 (reported by Shimizu Corporation) [2]. It can be observed from the distribution that the plane of the rupture or fault extends to about 500 km in the north-south direction (length) and about 200 km in the east-west direction (width).

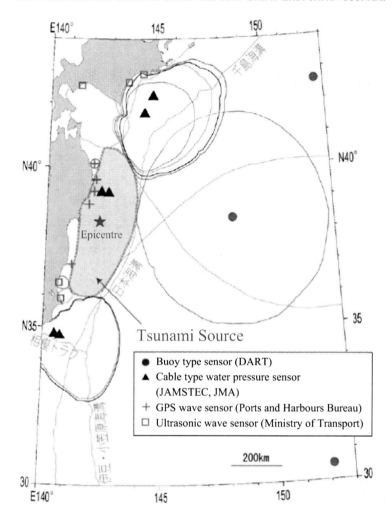

Figure 1: Tsunami source.

Before the main shock, an earthquake of magnitude 7.3 occurred in off-shore of the Sanriku region on March 9 (see Fig. 2). On the same day of the main event (11 March, 2011), 33 aftershocks were observed and their frequency decreased as days followed. Events with magnitude 7 or larger are summarized in Table 1. From the aftershocks, two events that occurred on 7th April and 11th April were of magnitude 7 and 7.1, respectively. These magnitudes led to emit the warning of tsunami occurrence. On the other hand, two large inland earthquakes occurred after the main shock. One occurred on 12th March in the northern part of Nagano Prefecture and was of magnitude 6.7. The other one was the earthquake of 15 March in the eastern part of Shizuoka Prefecture and it had a magnitude of 6.4. Also, an event of

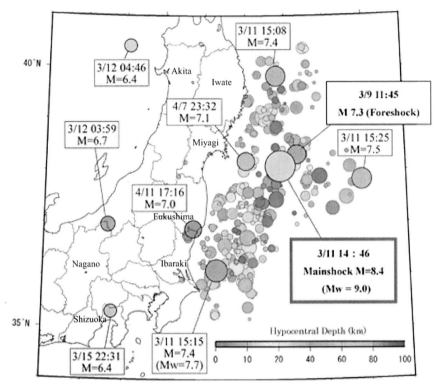

Figure 2: Distribution of epicentres.

Table 1: Main shock and events of large magnitude (larger than 7).

Event	Date and time	Epicentre	Depth (km)	Magnitude
Foreshock	03/09, 11:45	38°19.7′N, 143°16.7′E	8	Mj 7.3
Main	03/11, 14:46	38°06.2′N, 142°51.6′E	24	*Mw 9.0
Aftershocks	03/11, 15:08	39°50.3′N, 142°46.8′E	32	Mj 7.4
	03/11, 15:15	36°06.5′N, 141°15.9′E	43	Mj 7.7
	03/11, 15:25	37°50.2′N, 144°53.6′E	34	Mj 7.5
	04/07, 23:32	38°12.2′N, 141°55.2′E	66	Mj 7.1
	04/11, 17:16	36°56.7′N, 140°40.3′E	6	Mj 7.0

Abbreviations: Mj: Magnitude by Japan Meteorological Agency; *Mw: Moment Magnitude.

magnitude 6.4 in the northern part of Akita prefecture that falls out of the zone of aftershocks was observed. These events produced seismic intensities larger than 5 on the Japanese scale of earthquake intensity.

   Comparing Fig. 2 that is the distribution of aftershock epicentres and Fig. 1 that is the tsunami source region obtained by inverse analysis of tsunami observed data, it can be said that there is a good agreement between both figures. These results show that the earthquake of 11 March, 2011 with epicentre at 129 km west of the Sendai city has implied a rupture of a large geological fault that ranges from off the coast of Iwate prefecture to off the coast of Ibaraki prefecture, and therefore this event originated a great tsunami that affected cities located at the Pacific Ocean coast of the Tohoku region. The tsunami affected a wide area along the Pacific Ocean coastline from Hokkaido to the Kanto area. Tsunami waves were observed not only in the Hokkaido, Tohoku and Kanto regions, but also far regions such as Tokai, Shikoku and Kyushu regions. In Iwate prefecture and the northern area of Miyagi prefecture, the inundation height and the run-up height of tsunami exceeded 20 m. In Fig. 3, the distribution of the inundation height and run-up height is observed as is reported by the field survey carried out by the Building Research Institute, Ministry of Construction of Japan [3]. The small circles represent the inundation height that is the height between the water surface at the observation

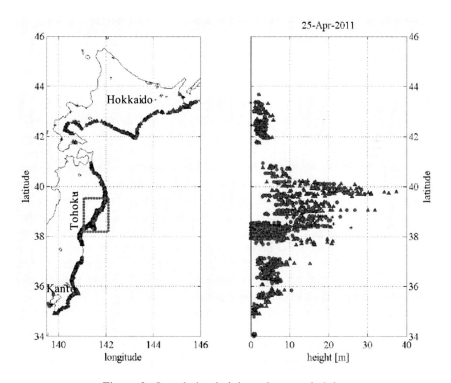

Figure 3: Inundation height and run-up heights.

point and the original or normal sea level. The triangles represent the run-up height that is the maximum topographical level reached by the tsunami in reference to the normal sea level. Since both heights are referred to the normal sea level (cero level), it does not mean that these heights are strictly related to the damages on structures. Instead of these heights, the inundation depth that is the height between the water surface at the observation point and the ground level at that point could be a better value to refer the damages of building. The inundation depth is more directly related to the water pressure that is the cause of the damages on the buildings. The inundation depth varies according to the topographical shape of the ground surface and during the field survey could be estimated from the marks of the tsunami that remains on taller building.

3 Damages due to tsunami

The damages, on building structures, that were produced by the tsunami are described in this section, specially the damages that occurred on reinforced concrete (RC) structures. However, it is necessary to mention that damages are not limited only to building structures. Tsunami also affected many infrastructures such as ports, embankments, roads, railroads, oil tanks and in its more dramatic damage affected the nuclear power plant of Fukushima. Environmental damages are also reported such as the chlorination of agricultural soils, sedimentation of debris near ports, transportation of old industrial and mine residues from the sea bottom to the ground surface, etc.

3.1 Selected area

The sites that were selected for this survey are shown in Fig. 4. This zone is also marked in Fig. 3 by a dashed rectangle. Cities of Ofunato, Rikuzentakata, Kesennuma, Ishinomaki and Onagawa were visited to perform the corresponding survey.

Figure 4 shows that the shape of the coast line is intricate with coast lines that converge forming shapes like river deltas that facilitate the run-up of tsunami. In the case of Ishinomaki city, as the location shows in the lower left corner of the figure, the coast line is straight; however, the large portion of the city is located parallel to this coast line and therefore the inundation area was large in comparison with other cities. On the other hand, high ground level in the Ishinomaki city is located far away of the coast line. Figure 5 is a detailed aerial photograph published by the Geospacial Information Authority of Japan (GSI) [4], where a portion of the Ishinomaki port after the tsunami can be located.

In Fig. 6, a portion of Ofunato city is shown. It is clear from the figure that only large building remains in the inundated zone while small building like wooden houses were washed up. These buildings were steel structures and RC structures that resist the lateral forces originated by the inundation of the tsunami. In the left part of Fig. 6, some intact constructions can be observed. These building are located on a high ground level that was not reached by the tsunami.

Figure 4: Zone of survey (Google map).

Figure 5: Details of the Ishinomaki city port affected by the tsunami.

Figure 6: Aerial photograph of Ofunato city after the tsunami.

In Fig. 7, a portion of the aerial photograph of Rikuzentaka city can be observed. Near the coast line only few buildings existed after the tsunami attack. The behaviour of the buildings located in the left part, which was a hotel, and the buildings of the lower right side that correspond to apartment buildings is described in the following section. It can be observed that the tsunami first destroyed a sea wall and then the sea water reached the road that can be observed as a straight line from the left to the lower right corner. On the right-upper corner by observing the colour of the vegetation the limit of the inundation area can be inferred. This place corresponds to a high ground level where a school building is located. These school facilities are now used as a shelter zone.

Figure 8 shows the condition of Onagawa town after the tsunami damage. In this aerial view it is possible to clearly identify the zones of high ground level by observing the condition of the vegetation. As can be observed in the figure, the area between the sea line and high ground level is narrow, and therefore the tsunami reached high inundation depths. This high level of water and poor soil condition originated the overturning of some RC buildings that is described in the following section.

Table 2 shows the extension of the inundated area and the number of family units in selected cities of this survey. The number of affected families and the extension of the inundated area are larger for Ishinomaki city. The extension of the inundation area was large due to the location of ports on lower ground along the coast line. On the other hand, Onagawa city is the zone with the smallest values; however, the

Figure 7: Aerial view of Rikuzentakata city after the tsunami.

Figure 8: Aerial view of Onagawa city after tsunami inundation.

Table 2: Inundated area and affected families in the investigated cities.

Prefecture	City	Inundated area (km^2)	Number of affected families
Iwate	Ofunato	8	6,957
	Rikuzentakata	13	5,592
Miyagi	Kesennuma	18	13,974
	Onagawa	3	3,155
	Ishinomaki	73	42,157

number of victims (deaths and disappeared) was of the order of 1000 persons (1/4 of the number of affected families) and in the case of Ishinomaki, victims reached 4000 persons (1/10 of the number of affected families). The high rate of victims of Onagawa city was due to the topographical condition of the location of the city with a very narrow area between the coast line and the surrounding hill. This condition led tsunami reach high inundation depths and it is also supposed that the successive waves of the tsunami produced violent flows of the sea water.

3.2 Damages on buildings

Damages on wooden structures and steel structures are described as reference to compare them with damages on RC buildings. In general, the wooden structures collapse when were attacked by the tsunami. The steel structures remain stand up however, the finishing walls, ceilings and other non-structural elements fail and in some cases these fails originate the damage of the main structure. The RC structures presented better behaviour and were the structures that in general remain in their original location without structural damages. This can be explained by the high lateral stiffness of RC buildings in comparison to steel structures and wooden structures. The wooden structures have smaller lateral stiffness and in general were washed up when the tsunami reached or covered the first floor. The relation between the damages and the earthquake resistant characteristics of these three types of structures is summarized in Table 3.

3.2.1 Damages on wooden houses

From damage surveys reported by other authors, it is recognized that in general the wooden houses collapse or present damages due to the tsunami action when the inundation depth is larger than 2 m. As is presented in Fig. 9, the damages on wooden houses are divided into three zones according to the inundation depth. Zone A corresponds to places where the inundation depth is smaller than 2 m and structural damages are not observed, that is the wooden houses are safe in this case. Zone B corresponds to a zone where the inundation zone ranges from 2 to 4 m, and depending on the structural shape, condition of the structural elements, etc. the houses can suffer from light damages to severe damages. From the field observation it can be said that when the water level cover the first floor of the

Table 3: Relation of earthquake-resistant forces and damages due to Tsunami.

Type of structure	Earthquake-resistant force for design	Level of tsunami damages
Wooden structure	Low	High
Steel structure	Medium	Medium
Reinforced concrete	High	Low

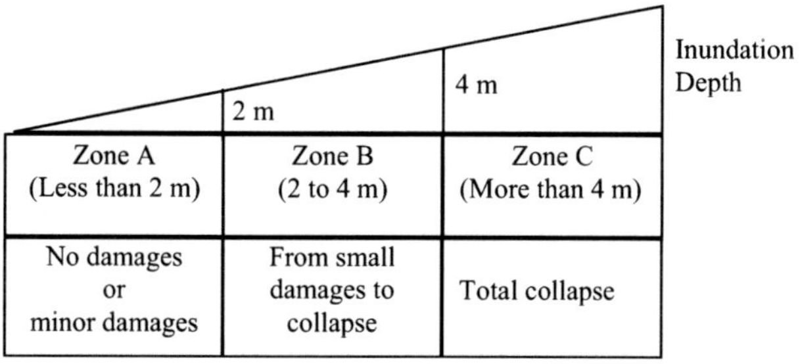

Zone A (Less than 2 m)	Zone B (2 to 4 m)	Zone C (More than 4 m)
No damages or minor damages	From small damages to collapse	Total collapse

2 m ... 4 m ... Inundation Depth

Figure 9: Inundation depth and damages on wooden houses.

wooden house, the structures collapse not only due to the lateral force of the water but also due to the water pressure on the ceiling of the first floor causing floating of the upper floors. Zone C corresponds to a zone where the inundation depth is larger than 4 m and total collapse of the structure is expected to occur.

Figure 10 shows some typical damages on wooden houses that were produced by the tsunami. In Fig. 10(a) it can be observed that wooden houses were completely destroyed by the tsunami action. It can be also observed that houses located on high sites are not affected. In Figs. 10(b) and (c) the first floor was destroyed by the tsunami and the upper parts of the houses were transported and then left by the tsunami on a different place from their original location. In the case of Fig. 10(d), the tsunami destroyed the first floor and also produced the overturning of the remaining upper floor.

3.2.2 Damages on steel structures

Steel structures are used in general for industrial facilities and office buildings. Most of the buildings are framed structures and structural elements such as beams and columns are slender elements. Floors and walls are made of light panels and the lateral stiffness is appropriately designed to resist the earthquake force. However during the tsunami attack the water pressure acting on panels or in general in elements of the large area generated large lateral forces that destroyed that non-structural elements, and in some cases the failure of these elements led to the failure and even to the collapse of the main structure.

Damages on steel structures can be observed in Fig. 11. When the inundation depth reaches only the first floor, the structure remains almost intact; however, the

Figure 10: Damages on wooden houses.

Figure 11: Damages on steel structures.

wall panels of the first floor suffer some damages as can be observed in Fig. 11(a). In Figs. 11(b) and (c) the inundation depth reached the second floor and wall panels and ceiling are destroyed. In this case, the structures remain stand up, however, some local failures of the structural elements were observed. Figure 11(d) shows a total collapse of steel structures. In this case, the building was completely covered by water.

3.2.3 Damages on RC structures

Many reinforced concrete structures resisted the tsunami action without collapse, as can be observed in Fig. 12. Figure 12(a) is the building of a local bank located at the Funato city, and it can be observed from the damage of the windows and the damage of the advertizement panel of the left corner of the building that the tsunami reached the third floor. In Fig. 12(b), it is also inferred that the tsunami covered the two-story building by observing that the windows glasses were destroyed and are now replaced by wood panels. Figure 12(c) is an apartment building located at Rikusentakata city and from the damages of the balconies it is inferred that the tsunami reached the fourth floor. Details of the damages of the balconies can be observed in Fig. 12(d), where the panels of the balconies of the fifth floor are intact while the panels of the lower floors are completed destroyed.

Figure 13 shows the condition of a hotel building located very near the shoreline in the Rikuzentakata city. The building resists the tsunami attack; however, the lower floors suffered the destruction of the non-structural elements and also, as is

Figure 12: RC buildings after tsunami attack.

Figure 13: Condition of the RC Building (hotel) near the shoreline.

Figure 14: Damages on reinforced concrete buildings.

observed in Fig. 13(a), the damage of a reinforced concrete wall due to the lateral water pressure. In this building, it was also observed that the cover concrete of structural elements of columns was spall-out probably due to a combination of earthquake vibration action and posterior tsunami, as can be observed in Fig. 13(b).

In general, reinforced concrete buildings did not collapse; however, under certain conditions the tsunami action caused the overturning and even the translation of building from its original location. This was reported by a survey team of the Tohoku Branch of the Architectural Institute of Japan [5] and the verification survey was carried out by the author. These damages occurred at Onagawa town and the affected buildings were those with weak foundation, and with shape like boxes that do not permit the transit of the water and facilitate the action of the floating force. In Fig. 14, damages of these buildings are shown.

Figure 14(a) shows an overturned three-story building with a shape of box and few openings. This building was completely covered by the tsunami water, and as is shown in Fig. 14(b) it has a shallow slab foundation that together with the shape of the building facilitates the action of the floating forces. Figure 14(c) shows the overturning of a two-story building with exposition of the pile foundation. Its use for lower rise buildings indicates the poor quality of the foundation ground. On the other hand in the Fig. 14(d) it can be observed that the building has suffered the impact of something (probably a ship) that could originate the overturning of the building.

4 Conclusions

Behaviour of RC building during the tsunami action originated by the Great East Japan Earthquake on 11 March, 2011 was discussed by comparing their damages with those of other type of constructions. Reinforced concrete buildings in general resist the tsunami without collapse; however, when constructions present shallow or weak foundation and building shapes induce the action of the floating force, overturning of the building was observed. In the case of non-collapsed buildings severe damages on non-structural elements such as panels and ceilings were observed.

If reinforced concrete buildings are intended to be used as refuge, buildings of more than four floors or more than 15 m are recommend. It is also important to check the condition of the foundation of the structures that are designated as refuge since the failure of the foundation could originate the overturning of the building. Additionally, this selected building must be verified to resist some impact forces or in any case must be located in places where the impact of displaced ships or other building can be avoided.

The survey has permitted to understand the behaviour of reinforced concrete buildings under tsunami attack and it can be state that these kind of buildings could be used to take refuge from tsunami in places where natural topography make impossible to reach hilltops or other safer places.

References

[1] Meteorological Research Institute, Japan Meteorological Agency. Report on the analysis results of Tohoku Pacific Earthquake of March 11, 2011 (in Japanese), available at http://www.mri-jma.go.jp/Topics/press/20110324/press20110324.html, 2011.
[2] Shimizu Corporation. Report on the Tohoku Area Pacific Offshore Earthquake, available at http://www.shimz.co.jp/english/theme/earthquake/outline.html, 2011.
[3] Building Research Institute, Ministry of Construction of Japan, survey team. Quick Report on the Tohoku Area Pacific Offshore Earthquake (in Japanese), 2011.
[4] Geospacial Information Authority of Japan (GSI). Aerial photographs of Tohoku region after the Great Earthquake of March 11, 2011 (in Japanese), available at http://saigai.gsi.go.jp/h23taiheiyo-ok/photo/photo_dj/index.html, 2011.
[5] Tohoku Branch of the Architectural Institute of Japan. Quick report of Tsunami damage at Onagawa town, March 29, 2011.

CHAPTER 6

Infrastructure maintenance and disaster prevention measures on Islands: example of the Izu Islands near Tokyo

H. Gotoh[1], M. Takezawa[1] & T. Murata[2]
[1]*Nihon University, Japan*
[2]*Tokyo Metropolitan Government*

Abstract

Of 6852 islands that make up the Japanese archipelago, 261 are isolated, inhabited islands with a total population of approximately 434,000 people concentrated in a total area of 5255 km^2. Within 5 years from 2001 to 2005, island population decreased by 8.3% compared to 0.7% increase in the national population. The Izu Island group, administered by the Tokyo Metropolitan Government, consists of nine separate islands: Izu-Ohshima, Toshima, Niijima, Shikinejima, Kouzushima, Miyakejima, Mikurajima, Hachijojima, and Aogashima. In 2009, the total population of the Izu Islands was 24,645, spread over a total area of 296.56 km^2. The largest island is Izu-Oshima (population: 8346, area: 91.06 km^2) and the smallest island is Toshima (population: 292, area: 4.12 km^2). The primary industries in the Izu Islands are fisheries, agriculture, and tourism, although the extent to which these are practiced varies between islands. Communication between various islands is by cargo-passenger boats, jetfoils, and aircrafts. While each island has a harbor or more, the five airports are on Izu-Ohshima, Niijima, Kouzushima, Miyakejima, and Hachijojima; the smaller islands can be reached by helicopter. In the event of tsunami, storm and flood damages, volcano eruption, etc. disaster prevention measures have been planned for each island by the Tokyo Metropolitan Government. These measures include supplying residents with hazard maps, refuge guidance, transport system for emergency supplies, simple sign, and radios. The present conditions, issues in future, and disaster prevention measures in the Izu Islands are discussed in this chapter.
Keywords: disaster prevention measure, isolated island, living standard, population

1 Introduction

The Japanese Archipelago, which forms the country of Japan, extends roughly from northeast to southwest along the northeastern coast of the Eurasia mainland, washing upon the northwestern shores of the Pacific Ocean. The archipelago consists of 6852 islands, including the four main islands (Honsyu, Hokkaido, Shikoku, and Kyusyu). Two hundred and sixty one isolated, inhabited islands of 6847 isolated islands excepted for Honsyu, Hokkaido, Shikoku, and Kyusyu from 6852 islands are designated by the Law for Development of Isolated Islands in Japan [1]. Isolated islands are almost far away from the mainlands where there are high buildings, cities, towns, etc. The area and the population of isolated, inhabited islands designated by the Law for Development of Isolated Islands in Japan [1] are about 5255 km^2 (1.39% vs. national area) and 434,000 persons (0.34% vs. national population). The isolated islands are surrounded by natural beauty and blessed with sightseeing and marine resources, and they also cover important roles of land and environmental preservation. Many isolated islands have possibility of territorial integrity as well as development. The culture of economic power, stable life, and public happiness is tried by executing various facilities based on isolated island politics every year. However, the remarkable difference of incomings and living standards between main lands and isolated islands remains in particular circumstance of isolated islands being surrounded by sea, a small area, and far away from the cultural center of mainland. This chapter discusses the infrastructure maintenance and the disaster prevention measures on isolated islands as an example of Izu Islands in the region of the Tokyo Metropolitan Government administratively in Japan.

2 Outlines of Izu Islands

The Izu Islands are oceanic islands and a chain of volcanic islands scattered over several hundred kilometers south of Tokyo, Japan as shown in Figs. 1 and 2 [2]. The Izu Islands are a group of volcanic islands stretching south and east from the Izu Peninsula of Honsyu, Japan. Administratively, they form two towns and six villages. The largest is Izu Oshima, usually called simply Ohshima. Although traditionally referred to as the "Izu Seven," there are in fact more than a dozen islands and islets. Nine out of them are currently inhabited. The total administrated area of the Izu Islands is about 301.56 km^2 and is home to 24,242 people in 2005. All the islands lie within the Fuji-Hakone-Izu National Park. Each of Izu Ohshima and Hachijojima forms two towns. The remaining seven islands form six villages, with Niijima and Shikinejima forming one village. Three subprefectures (Ohshima, Miyake, and Hachijo) are formed above the municipalities as branch offices of the Tokyo metropolitan government. Volcanic activity is frequent in the area. The Eruption of Myoujin-shou in 1953 killed 31 people when the research vessel Kaiyou Maru No. 5 was destroyed.

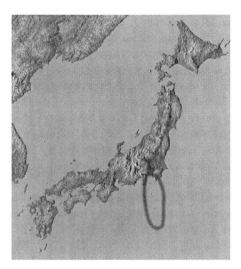

Figure 1: Japan Islands.

Figure 2: Izu Islands.

Volcanic activity, including the release of harmful gases, forced the evacuation of Miyakejima in 2000. In February 2005, residents were allowed to return permanently to the island but were required to carry gas masks in the case of future volcanic emissions. The Izu Islands lie southeast of mainland Tokyo in Pacific Ocean. The closest, Izu-Ohshima, is 108 km away, while Aogashima is 354 km away from the Tokyo Metropolitan Office. Each island is unique, in which it has its own character and all sorts of marine sports such as swimming, scuba diving, surfing, and fishing can be enjoyed. There are many places that offer scenic beauty, which are crowded with tourists during the summer. These are the islands found in a fairly straight line from the southeastern shore of the Izu Peninsula to the south. They are islands popular as marine resorts where you can enjoy activities such as fishing and diving. All the Izu Islands offer their own unique features such as Izu-Ohshima famous for Mt. Mihara (active volcano) and Izu-Ohshima camellias, Hachijojima with its history as a penal colony, and Mikurajima where dolphin watching can be enjoyed. The fauna and flora have gone through their own evolution since the islands are isolated from the mainland. Therefore, you will find an ecosystem that is rare and unique. Dolphins and whales live in the nearby sea, attracting many tourists who enjoy watching these sea mammals. These are the inhabited islands of the Izu Islands on the Honsyu (mainland) side. Generally, Izu-Ohshima, Toshima, Niijima, Kouzushima, Miyakejima, Hachijojima, and Mikurajima are considered as the seven islands but sometimes Shikinejima and Aogashima are also included. Each of these islands are extremely characteristic such as Ohshima famous for Mt. Mihara and Ohshima camellias, Niijima with its many beautiful beaches, Kouzushima with its amazing white sandy shores, Miyakejima once again being gradually visited by tourists after evacuation orders due to volcanic eruption have been lifted, and Hachijojima where its one-of-a-kind culture featuring textiles and performing art is preserved. These islands are blessed with lush greenery and beautiful sea and are popular leisure spots where you can enjoy diving, surfing, bird watching, and trekking [2]. The Tokyo Metropolitan Government proposed the Promotion Plan of Isolated Island in Tokyo over 10 years (2003–2012) in 2003 [3]. The basic policy is the independent development of Izu Islands based on having all in all to nation common property in space of valuable healing. Izu Islands with Ogasawara Islands secure about 45% of Exclusive Economic Zone in Japan. The important policy of the Promotion Plan is the establishment of an island based on the tourism that is sightseeing cooperated with agriculture and fishery, synthetic network of communication in viewpoint of visitors, intensification of highly information and communication bases, and establishment of the crisis management system. Besides, the maintenance of life environments, medical institutions, welfare facilities, educational institutions, cultural properties, etc. are planned and executed in Izu Islands at present. Moreover, The Public Corporation of Promotion in Izu and Ogasawara Islands was established by the foundation of the Tokyo Metropolitan Government and the communities of islands in 1998 [4]. The main businesses are the sales drive of special products in each island, the supports of the navigation among each island by the heli-commuter (see Figs. 3–16) [5].

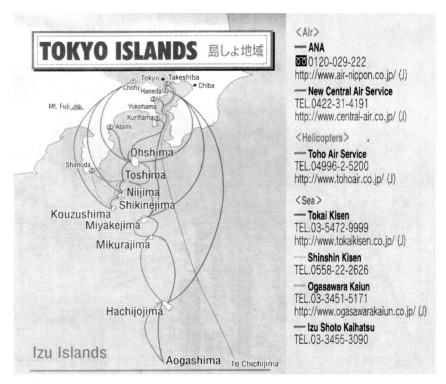

Figure 3: Traffic network from Tokyo Metropolitan to Izu Islands.

Figure 4: Jetfoil (high-speed boat). 1 h 45 min (from Tokyo to Ohshima), 2 h
50 min to 3 h 40 min (from Tokyo to Niijima, Shikinejima, Kouzushima),
45 min to 1 h (from Atami, Kurihama, Tateyama to Ohshima).

Figure 5: Boat ride. 8 h (from Tokyo to Ohshima), 9 h 40 min to 11 h 10 min. (from Tokyo to Toshima, Niijima, Shikinejima, Kouzushima, Mikurajima, and Hachijojima).

Figure 6: Air plane. 25–35 min (from Tokyo to Ohshima), 35–40 min (from Tokyo to Niijima, Kouzushima, Miyakejima, and Hachijojima).

Figure 7: Helicopter. 10–25 min (from Ohshima to Toshima, Miyakejima, Mikurajima, Hachijojima, and Aogashima).

Figure 8: Ohshima (33.733°N, 139.4°E).

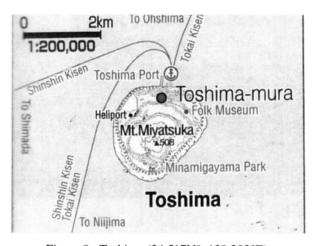

Figure 9: Toshima (34.517N°, 139.283°E).

Figure 10: Niijima(34.367°N, 139.267°E).

Figure 11. Shikinejima(34.325°N,139.217°E).

Figure 12: Kouzushima(34.217°N,139.15°E).

Figure 13: Miyakejima (34.083°N, 139.533°E).

Figure 14: Mikurajima (33.875°N, 139.6°E).

Figure 15: Hachijojima (33.117°N, 139.783°E).

Figure 16: Aogashima (31.88°N, 139.92°E).

3 Population, aging, and industrial structures of Izu Islands

Izu Islands have been losing population every year. Table 1 shows changes of Izu Islands, isolated islands, and national population in Japan [6].

Table 2 shows changes of population in towns and villages of Izu Islands in 2000 and 2005, where the population of Miyakejima in 2000 is before the eruption of Mt. Oyama, and the population and the area of Shikinejima are contained in those of Niijima [6].

Table 3 shows the age group of Izu Islands in 2005, where the age group of Shikinejima is contained in that of Niijima [6].

The industrial structures of Izu Islands were the primary industry 12%, the secondary industry 22%, and the tertiary industry 66% on average in 2005. Employers of agriculture and fishery in the primary industry and employees of construction, manufacture, and mining in the secondary industry in 2005 have been decreasing compared with those in the past, but employers of information, transport, accommodation, real estate, and living-relation in the tertiary industry in 2005 have been increasing every year. The industry of Izu Islands is mainly fishery, agriculture, and sightseeing though they vary at each island. For example, the sightseeing is the support of Izu-Ohshima, Niijima, Miyakejima, and Mikurajima, agriculture and forestry of the camellia is a prosperous business at Toshima, fishery is famous at Kouzushima, and animal husbandry of milking cows is the basic industry at Aogashima. Hachijojima is popular among surfers, and scuba diving points are many and varied. Hachijojima is also known for its natural hot spring, hiking, waterfalls, and natural beauty. Table 4 is industrial structures of each island in 2005 [6].

Table 1: Changes of population (persons).

Year	Izu islands	Isolated island	National
1960	38,707	923,062	94,301,623
1970	32,539	736,712	104,665,171
1980	31,902	630,536	117,060,396
1990	30,032	546,505	123,611,167
2000	28,756	472,312	126,925,843
2005	26,242	433,712	127,767,994

Table 2: Changes of population in Izu islands.

Town or village	2000 (persons)	2005 (persons)	Area (km^2)
Izu-Ohshima	9549	8702	91.06
Toshima	297	308	4.12
Niijima	3180	3161	27.83
Kouzushima	2263	2068	18.87
Miyakejima	3783	2439	55.50
Hachijojima	9305	8837	77.62
Mikurajima	258	292	20.58
Aogashima	193	214	5.98

Table 3: Age group of Izu islands.

Town or Village	0–14 years old (%)	15–64 years old (%)	Above 65 years old (%)
Izu-Ohshima	12.0	59.9	28.1
Toshima	10.6	66.7	22.8
Niijima	11.9	56.8	31.3
Kouzushiima	14.9	60.7	24.4
Miyakejima	5.7	56.4	37.9
Mikurajima	16.5	69.2	14.3
Hachijojima	12.7	58.3	29.0
Aogashima	20.2	65.2	14.6

Table 4: Industrial structures of each island.

Island	Primary (%)	Secondary (%)	Third (%)
Izu-Ohshima	8	16	76
Toshima	21	19	60
Niijima (Contain Shikinejima)	7	23	68
Kouzushima	19	14	67
Miyakejima	6	25	69
Mikurajima	2	25	73
Hachijojima	19	17	64
Aogashima	10	36	54

4 Land uses, infrastructures, and tourism of Izu Islands

At present the natural land is about 86%, the urban district is about 8% (contained the residential area 4%), and the farmland is about 6% in Izu Islands. The trend of land uses is that the residential area is increasing and the forest is decreasing every year. Of the residential area, the independent houses and the educational culture facilities are increasing, but the facility of agriculture, forestry and fishery, accommodation, playground, and apartment are decreasing every year. The ratio of land use at each island of Izu Island is shown in Table 5 [7].

The land use division of the residential area at each islands is shown in Table 6 [7]. The land use of houses is 40–60% at many islands excepted for Aogashima.

There are 5 airports, 15 harbors, and 19 fishing ports in Izu Islands. Three airlines are navigated at about 30 min to 1 h between Haneda (Tokyo International Airport) and Izu Ohshima, Miyakejima, Hachijojima, and three commuter airlines are navigated at about 30 min to 1 h between Choufu air port and Izu-Oshima, Niijima, Kouzushima. Also, there are regular heli-commuter (commuter airline of helicopter) services between Aogashima, Hachijojima, Mikurajima, Miyakejima, Izu-Ohshima, and Toshima. There are some liners between Honsyu (Tokyo, Yokohama, Atami, Shimoda) and Izu Islands. Though the required time between Tokyo and Izu Island is 7–10 h by liners, the high-speed jet foils navigates at about 2 h between Tokyo and Izu-Oshima. Annual visitors to Izu Island was about 1,000,000 persons in 1980, but they decreased to about 450,000 visitors in 2008 [8–10]. Tables 7 and 8 are the facilities of airports and the availability in Izu Islands. Tables 9 and 10 are facilities of harbors and fishing harbors in Izu Island [11].

Upper is in 2011 and lower (   ) is in 2008.

Table 5: The ratio of land use (%).

	A	B	C	D	E	F	G	H	I	J
(1)	5.3	0.6	0.9	0.2	2.9	4.7	0.1	64.3	21.1	14.7
(2)	3.2	0.5	0.5	0.1	3.4	2.2	0.1	67.8	22.3	9.9
(3)	4.6	3.2	1.1	0.3	3.2	2.7	0.1	72.0	12.8	15.2
(4)	2.5	0.7	0.2	0.3	4.0	10.7	0.2	54.6	26.8	18.6
(5)	2.8	0.4	0.1	0.2	2.4	4.5	0.3	77.5	11.8	10.7
(6)	0.4	0.1	0.1	0.0	0.7	1.4	0.0	84.2	13.0	2.8
(7)	5.2	0.5	0.6	0.8	4.5	12.8	0.2	71.4	4.1	24.4
(8)	2.0	0.9	0.2	0.9	2.0	10.3	0.0	57.1	26.7	16.2
(9)	3.8	0.8	0.6	0.3	2.9	6.0	0.1	71.5	14.1	14.5

(1) Izu-Ohshima, (2) Toshima, (3) Niijima, (4) Kouzushima, (5) Miyakejima, (6) Mikurajima,
(7) Hachijojima, (8) Aogashima, and (9) Isu Islands
A: Residential area, B: Other use area of outdoor, C: Park, D: Nonuse area, E: Road, F: Farmland,
G: Water surface, H:. Forest, I: Field, J: Other than forest and field.

Table 6: The ratio of the residential area use (%).

	Public	Commerce	House	Industry	Farming
(1)	19.1	10.8	63.7	4.1	2.3
(2)	30.1	9.9	43.5	12.7	3.8
(3)	20.5	16.3	44.3	12.2	6.6
(4)	23.1	20.2	38.2	14.8	3.7
(5)	15.6	15.5	54.5	8.6	5.8
(6)	26.2	9.2	46.8	11.5	6.2
(7)	13.5	16.2	58.2	7.1	5.1
(8)	45.0	7.5	28.2	11.4	7.8
(9)	19.9	12.4	57.9	6.5	3.3

(1) Izu-Ohshima, (2) Toshima, (3) Niijima, (4) Kouzushima, (5) Miyakejima, (6) Mikurajima,
(7) Hachijojima, (8) Aogashima, and (9) Isu Islands

Table 7: Facilities of airports.

Airport	Ohshima	Miyakejima	Hachijojima	Niijima	Kouzushima
Field length (m)	1800	1200	2000	800	800
Apron (m^2)	20,525	8350	15,300	3000	3000
Terminal building (m^2)	2643	491	3975	610	586

Table 8: Availability of airlines.

	Haneda–Ohshima	Haneda–Miyakejima	Haneda–Hachijojima	Choufu–Ohshima	Choufu–Niijima	Choufu–Kouzushima
(1)	344 (630)	115 (136)	1002 (1378)	1007 (987)	1327 (1244)	892 (963)
(2)	11,548 (41,294)	5,469 (8,863)	186,150 (200,045)	19,317 (16,400)	26,771 (24,494)	17,414 (16,766)
(3)	52,214 (107,521)	41 (235)	1,386,526 (2,462,240)	17,790 (4982)	31,423 (34,421)	1373 (3007)

(1) Number of flight served by airplane (1round trip flight).
(2) Number of passenger (persons).
(3) Flight flows (kg).

Table 9: Facilities of harbors.

Harbor	Vessels	Facility	
Ohshima(Motomachi)	500–5000 (ton)	Quay	460 m
	(small ship)	Wharf	50 m
		Waiting room 1 (block)	
Ohshima (Okada)	500–5000 (ton)	Quay	430 m
		Waiting room 1 (block)	
Ohshima (Habu)	4000 (ton)	Quay	135 m
		Wharf	757 m
		Slipway	1290 m^2
Toshima	500–5000 (ton)	Quay	410 m
	(small ship)	Wharf	137 m
		Slipway	2400 m^2
		Waiting room 1 (block)	
Niijima	500–5000 (ton)	Quay	380 m
	(small ship)	Wharf	299 m
		Slipway	2400 m^2
		Waiting room 1 (block)	
Shikinejima	5000 (ton)	Quay	150 m
	(small ship)	Wharf	80 m
		Slipway	3675 m^2
		Waiting room 1 (block)	
Kouzushima	500–5000 (ton)	Quay	440 m
	(small ship)	Wharf	617 m
		Slipway	7510 m^2
		Waiting room 1 (block)	
Miyakejima (Miike)	500–5000 (ton)	Quay	230 m
		Waiting room 1 (block)	
Miyakejima (Okubo)	Small ship	Wharf	30 m
Mikurajima	5000 (ton)	Quay	300 m
	(small ship)	Wharf	232 m
		Slipway	2335 m^2
Hachijojima (Kaminato)	500–5000(ton)	Quay	310 m
		Slipway	1320 m^2
		Waiting room 1 (block)	
Hachijyojima (Yaene)	500–5000 (ton)	Quay	230 m
Aogashima (Aogashima)	(Small ship)	Wharf	54 m
		Slipway	588 m^2
		Waiting room 1 (block)	
Aogashima (Ochiyo)	(Small ship)	Wharf	50 m

Table 10: Facilities of fishing harbor.

Harbor	Breakwater (m)	Quay/wharf (m)	Slipway (m^2)
Ohshima (Motomachi)	568	187	3460
Ohshima (Okada)	330	284	4452
Ohshima (Nomasu)	349	140	2253
Ohshima (Sashikiji)	255	111	1720
Ohshima (Izumitsu)	149	90	2456
Niijima (Wakago)	836	544	4916
Niijima (Habushi)	357	450	1600
Shikinejima (Nobushi)	203	575	2004
Shikinejima (Ohama)	128	203	2756
Kouzushima (Miura)	793	834	2600
Miyakejima (Yunohama)	252	210	2317
Miyakejima (Igaya)	240	298	2625
Miyakejima (Okubo)	357	101	1800
Miyakejima (Tsubota)	654	435	4051
Miyakejimaq (Ago)	202	1060	3090
Hachijojima (Dorinsawa)	544	229	3315
Hachijojima (Nakanogo)	251	105	3748
Hachijojima (kaminato)	598	921	5394
Hachijojima (Yaene)	685	752	4455

The transport facility on Izu Islands is by bus, car, the motorbike, bicycle, etc. Therefore, the road takes an important role on promotions and cultivations of various industries and the life of inhabitants in Izu Islands. Total lengths of main roads paved are about 215 km versus land areas about 300 km^2 of Izu Islands [8–10].

Most of Izu Islands carried out the life of lump because there was no electricity before 1953. The electricity coverage of Izu Islands was 98% since 1962 [8–10].

Social welfare facilities of Izu Islands are seated by special nursing homes for the aged (number of persons admitted 750), home care service centers for the aged of each town and village, community comprehensive support center of each town and village, life support house for the aged, rehabilitation facilities for physically challenged persons in mental, private facilities for physically challenged persons in mind and body, living houses for physically challenged persons in mind, home support center for children, and community welfare center, etc. of Izu Islands. Under medical facilities there are 18 clinics and 1 hospital; 30 doctors are staying in Izu Islands. There are 14 sental offices in Izu Islands. There are 18 nursery schools with 1000 students. Educational institutes include 15 elementary schools (number of schoolchildren 1150), 13 junior high schools (number of students 600), and 8 high schools (number of students 750) in Izu Islands [12].

The Izu Islands are a group of volcanic islands in the Fuji Volcanic Belt that stretches from north to south for about 540 km. The group consists of Izu Ohshima, Toshima, Niijima, Shikinejuma, Kouzushima, Miyakejima, Mikurajima, Hachijo-jima, and Aogashima islands, and is a part of Fuji Hakone Izu National Park. It is administratively a part of Tokyo. Izu-Ohshima, the largest of all the islands, is famous for its flora, such as camellias and azaleas. It is a popular resort area with moderate climate, a fantastic view of Mt. Mihara, and "anko" (the type of clothing worn by local women). Flocks of brown boobies live in Toshima. Niijima is famous for the scenery at Hanebushi-ura Inlet along its east coast. Shikinejima has a number of secluded beaches, hot springs, shrines, and temple. Kouzushi-ma's geographical features are intricate, and there are many historical ruins of temples and shrines on the island. Miyakejima is famous for camellias and hydrangeas. The entire Mikurajima is a vast virgin forest of box trees and chin-quapins. Hachijojima has wonderful subtropical scenery. Aogashima is famous for the festival of cattle. Each island welcomes many visitors every year. All of the islands are surrounded by the beautiful ocean, and visitors can enjoy fishing, surf-ing, diving, and many other types of marine sports. Dolphin watching is becoming more and more popular in recent years. As they are volcanic islands, there are plenty of hot springs to be found there as [8–10]. The Promotion Plan of Isolated Island in Tokyo over 10 years (2003–2012) [3] was announced by the Tokyo Metropolitan Government in 2003 and the keynote was the establishment of an island based on the tourism that is sightseeing cooperated with agriculture and fishery, synthetic network of communication in viewpoint of visitors, intensifica-tion of highly information and communication bases, and establishment of crisis management system. Besides, the maintenance of life environments, medical institutions, welfare facilities, educational institutions, cultural properties, etc. is planned and executed in Izu Islands at present. Following was the plan for each island: Izu-Ohshima for the promotion of sustainable tourism cooperated with agriculture, fishery, and tourism; Toshima for steadiness and improvement of pro-ductions attempted by a systematic farming and a managing fishery; Niijima and Shikinejima were for the impulsion of tourism through experiences that exploit the nature of island over the cooperation of the agriculture, fishery, and tourism with a healing program exploiting the spa under the sea for securing visitors through a year; Kouzushima for promotion of the tourism to make use of the nature cooperating with the fishery, and aimed to form a healthy island for relax-ation and a healing; Miyakejima positioned the grand plan of the area promotion for tourism and took actively a sensible approach for conservation of nature over relating with the tourism and the other industries of fishery, agriculture, forestry, etc.; Mikurajima planned to activate the island on the basic policy for promoting tourism of favorable environment in nature; Hachijojima has promoted the tour-ism through experience being able to enjoy the bare truth of the island with exploiting actively the area resources and training synthetically the agriculture, fishery, and tourism; and Aogashima has activated the economy of the island by strengthening and supplying regular sea foods and marine product of brand-name goods and special products.

5 Living standards and environmental hygiene in Izu Islands

The living standard is the level of comfort and wealth that people have. It has been investigated by the Asahi Newspaper Company that the energy (Minryoku) [13] that people have in the field of production, expenditure, culture, life, etc. is given by 10 indices of population I_P, number of household I_H, income cost subjected to taxation I_I, number of employees I_E, produced cost of agriculture I_A, annual shipped cost of industrial products I_S, annual selling cost of retailer I_R, deposit account I_D, number of automobile I_C, and number of television contractors I_T. Table 11 is the index of human energy at each island of Izu Islands in 2000–2005, where the index of human energy at Shikinejima is contained in Niijima.

Each index of human energy is calculated as follows: for example, the index of population I_P is $I_P = \{(\text{population of each area})/(\text{national population})\} \times 100,000$,

where 100,000 is the national index, and also the annual shipped cost of industrial products I_S and the annual selling cost of retailer I_R are calculated by each of weight 22 and 47. Consequently, the index of human energy I is calculated by

$$I = \{I_P + I_H + I_I + I_E + (I_A + 22I_S + 47I_R)/70 + I_D + I_C + I_T\}/8$$

Moreover, the index I_B of human energy per a person is obtained by $I_B = I/I_P$
Table 12 shows changes of I_B, where the national average is $I_B = 100$.

Table 11: Index of human energy.

Year	2000	2001	2002	2003	2004	2005
Ohshima	7.6	7.6	7.6	7.9	7.5	7.2
Toshima	0.3	0.3	0.3	0.3	0.3	0.3
Niijima	2.6	2.5	2.4	2.5	2.7	2.7
Kouzushima	1.6	1.6	1.5	1.6	1.6	1.7
Miyakejima	3.2	3.2	2.5	2.5	2.2	3.3
Mikurajima	0.2	0.2	0.2	0.2	0.2	0.2
Hachijojima	7.5	7.5	7.8	7.8	7.5	7.3
Aogashima	0.2	0.2	0.2	0.2	0.2	0.2

Table 12: Changes of I_B.

Year	2000	2001	2002	2003	2004	2005
Ohshima	100.0	101.3	102.0	107.7	103.5	100.4
Toshima	150.0	150.0	129.3	109.3	124.6	124.4
Niijima	104.0	100.0	97.1	102.5	108.4	109.3
Kouzushima	88.9	88.9	85.3	90.5	94.8	99.3
Miyakejima	106.7	106.7	84.6	87.6	81.1	126.9
Mikurajima	100.0	100.0	90.7	95.0	91.7	101.0
Hachijojima	101.4	101.4	106.5	107.2	104.8	102.4
Aogashima	100.0	100.0	126.3	113.1	116.7	115.7

Each island except for Kouzushima is that the index of human energy per 1 person is 100 or over in 2000–2005. Though the index of human energy per person in the center of Tokyo is about 300; indices of human energy at other isolated islands are $I_B = 80$–95.

There are environmental hygiene facilities of 40 barber shops, 49 beauty salons, 13 laundry shops, 31 public bathhouses, etc.

The water must be saved with each island. The inhabitants of each island were depended on the rain water for a long time, but the small-scale water works have been expanded since 1953. The coverage of water service arrives at 99% and over in 2008. However, the water charge of Izu Islands is higher than one of the main land because of being necessary for construction costs and public loans accompanied with small-scale water works. Garbage collection and disposal were dumped at coast, stream, etc. or incinerated at garden, yard, etc. by each home before the late 1960s. Refuse incinerators were set in each town and village from 1961–1975. Collections of garbage by their types are carried out by delegated dealers at present. The human waste is treated by pump up and sewage disposal facilities at any time [8–10].

6 Disaster prevention measures

In Tokyo, tsunami may strike at island areas due to a major earthquake. Niijima, Kouzushima, and Miyakejima are designated as areas that have a possibility of being affected by tsunami due to a Tokai region (34.5°N, 137°E and 139°E) earthquake. The Tokai earthquakes are major earthquakes that have occurred regularly with an interval of 100 to 150 years in the Tokai region of Japan. The Tokai segment has been struck by earthquakes in 1498, 1605, 1707, and 1854. Hachijojima is designated as an area that has a possibility of being affected by tsunami due to a Tonankai and Nankai region earthquake. The Tonankai earthquake occurred on 7 December, 1944. It had an estimated magnitude of 8.1 on the moment magnitude scale. It triggered a large tsunami that caused serious damage along the Pacific coast of Wakayama Prefecture (33.5°N, 136°E) and the Tokai region (34.5°N, 137°E and 139°E). Together the earthquake and tsunami caused 1223 casualties. The Nankai earthquakes (33°N, 133°E to 135°E) are great earthquakes that occur along the fault that forms the plate interface between the subducting Philippine Sea Plate and the overriding Amurian Plate (part of the Eurasian Plate), which dips beneath southwestern Honshu, Japan. The 1923, Great Kanto earthquake struck the Kanto plain (35°N, 139.5°E) on the Japanese main island of Honsyu on September 1, 1023. The quake had a magnitude of 8.2 on the Richter scale, with its focus deep beneath Izu-Ohshima Island in Sagami Bay. All of these great earthquakes have given rise to damaging tsunami. Main tsunami earthquakes of Izu-Ohshima Islands that occurred in the past are as follows: In 1498, tsunami height 2.6 m in Niijima, 3.1 m in Shikinejima, and 4.0 m in Hachijojima were recorded, and one cargo handler at a harbor drowned in Hachijojima. In 1605, 37 people were died at Tanigasato in Hachijojima by tsunami height 10–20 m. In 1677, wave runs up to Tanigasato by tsunami height 3–4 m in Hachijojima, and one person died and about 10 fisher boats were flowed out by tsunami of 3 height m in Aogashima. In 1703, 56 people died and 58 houses and 18 ships flowed out at Okada in Ohshima. In 1707, tsunami height was 4 m in Hachijojima. In 1854, tsunami height was 3 m in Ohshima; in 1923, tsunami height was 12 m at Okada in Ohshima; in 1953, tsunami height was 0.34 m in Ohshima and 1.5 m in Hachijojima. In 1960, the tsunami height was 1.0. To prevent tsunami disasters, the Tokyo Metropolitan Government investigated the potential for tsunami flooding islands areas. Tsunami flooding prediction of Izu-Island was carried out on four cases of assuming Tokai earthquake (case 1), assuming Tonankai/Nankai earthquake (case 2), interaction assuming Tokai earthquake and assuming Tonankai/Nankai earthquake (case 3), and assuming Kanto earthquake (case 4). The calculation range was from below Honsyu/Shikoku/the pacific of Kyushu to at 26.5°N, and from 131°E to 142.5°E. The condition for calculation was started in 1280 m mesh, and calculated in 10 m mesh for important areas around the coastal areas. Calculation time is 12 h after an earthquake occurs. Table 13 shows the results of tsunami simulation [14].

In order to respond promptly and consistently to emergencies, the Tokyo Metropolitan Government created a special management association with work on establishing a crisis management system to gather and analyze information and prepare strategic measures. The Tokyo Metropolitan Government established a disaster prevention system with the Disaster Countermeasure Headquarters as its center and deals with disasters with the national government, municipalities, and other agencies based on information from the Disaster Prevention Center. During a catastrophic disaster, initial responses will keep damage from spreading. The Tokyo Metropolitan Government has established the following initial response measures. To respond at night and during holidays, the center has an after-hours communication office and accommodations for disaster management staff. Also, it installed emergency government wireless systems to secure a system to collect and deliver information, seismometer network, supervisory video cameras, and a disaster information system to organize disaster information. In the event of a catastrophic disaster, the Tokyo Metropolitan Government had set up "Tokyo Metropolitan Government Disaster Countermeasure Headquarters" (headed by the governor of Tokyo) to discuss various measures including information gathering, fire fighting, first-aid/rescue, etc. and implement them [15]. Izu Islands observe typhoons every year. Therefore, each of Izu Islands suffered a lot of strong wind or heavy rainfall throughout the year. Also, on Izu Islands series of frequent earthquakes have been happening in the past. The Japanese government designates to the fortified area of disaster measure for earthquakes The Tokyo Metropolitan Government prepared a report of the predicted research on the inundation due to Tsunami of Izu Islands in 2004 [3] and planned the disaster prevention measures of Izu Islands for the flood damages and the earthquakes in 2006 [15]. Each of Izu Islands endeavors to stockpile preserved foods, clothing, carpets, etc. based on the disaster ordinance of the Tokyo Metropolitan Government. Besides, the adjustment on the navigation of the emergency helicopter is practiced and the improvement of the emergency services is strengthened for the safety of the inhabitants. In addition, the administrative radio of the disaster was established in 1970, and the

Table 13: Tsunami height and concentration time.

Island	Case 1	Case 2	Case 3	Case 4
Ohshima	0.71 m	0.81 m	0.92 m	3.38 m
(Okada)	20.3 min	22.2 min	21.1 min	4.3 min
Ohshima	1.23 m	1.45 m	1.45 m	1.75 m
(Motomachi)	17.8 min	14.5 min	14.5 min	4.1 min
Ohshima	0.49 m	0.79 m	0.97 m	0.45 m
(Habu)	21.4 min	21.6 min	17.9 min	7.6 min
Ohshima	0.30 m	0.53 m	0.50 m	2.83m
(Senzu)	22.2 min	22.6 min	20.8 min	3.2 min
Toshima	0.85 m	1.08 m	1.40 m	1.93 m
	11.7 min	14.9 min	14.1 min	11.5 min
Niijima	2.19 m	1.52 m	2.61 m	1.50 m
(Niijima)	14.6 min	15.3 min	13.5 min	17.4 min
Niijima	2.19 m	1.52 m	2.61 m	1.50 m
(Wakago)	14.6 min	15.3 min	13.5 min	17.4 min
Shikinejima	2.14 m	2.66 m	3.37 m	1.35 m
(Shikinejima)	14.1 min	14.7 min	14.0 min	7.6 min
Shikinejima	2.14 m	2.66 m	3.37 m	1.35 m
(Nobushi)	14.1 min	14.7 min	14.0 min	7.6 min
Kouzushima	2.14 m	2.45 m	3.37 m	0.72 m
	10.1 min	11.5 min	10.7 min	9.5 min
Miyakejima	1.55 m	1.70 m	1.98 m	0.60 m
(Miike)	22.3 min	16.5 min	16.7 min	17.1 min
Miyakejima	1.31 m	2.56 m	2.50 m	0.80 m
(Okubo)	23.2 min	16.5 min	12.8 min	17.9 min
Miyakejima	1.56 m	3.08 m	3.64 m	0.82 m
(Igaya)	22.3 min	13.9 min	13.9 min	8.4 min
Miyakejima	0.91 m	1.41 m	1.61 m	0.47 m
(Ako)	19.6 min	11.9 min	12.0 min	20.7 min
Miyakejima	1.09 m	1.59 m	1.68 m	0.54 m
(Tsubota)	20.5 min	14.9 min	10.4 min	17.9 min
Mikurajima	1.02 m	1.23 m	1.24 m	0.53 m
	18.3 min	11.0 min	6.8 min	18.8 min
Hachijojima	0.95 m	3.26 m	3.44 m	0.49 m
(Yaene)	25.1 min	23.8 min	23.6 min	21.3 min
Hachijojima	1.04 m	1.98 m	1.85 m	0.50 m
(Kaminato)	25.4 min	24.4 min	24.3 min	23.6 min
Hachijojima	0.45 m	2.04 m	2.33 m	0.52 m
(Borawazawa)	30.5 min	29.7 min	29.6 min	25.1 min
Hachijojima	0.34 m	1.70 m	1.72 m	0.33 m
(Nakanogo)	25.5 min	23.4 min	23.4 min	22.8 min
Aogashima	0.24 m	2.43 m	2.44 m	0.18 m
	29.8 min	27.5 min	27.6 min	39.7 min

information system of disaster in Tokyo Metropolitan Government was innovated in 1991. Consequently, it was able to communicate the information of disaster between the disaster center of the Tokyo Metropolitan Government and each of Izu Islands. Furthermore, equipments of communication were renewed in 2008. Another disaster prevention measure of Izu Islands is the volcanic eruption. Izu Ohshima is most famous for Mt. Mihara that last erupted in 1986. Also, Mt. Oyama of Miyakejima has erupted several times in the recent past. A lava flow in 1940 killed 11 people, and other eruptions occurred in 1962 and 1983. On July 14, 2000, Mt. Oyama began another series of eruptions, and by September, the island was completely evacuated. After a 4-year period of volcanic emissions, residents were allowed to return permanently on February 1, 2005. After the eruption, there has been a constant flow of sulfuric gas coming from Mt. Oyama. Message dials of disaster after eruption of Mt. Oyama in 2000 were supplied and 6 mG radio system of Izu Islands was serviced in 2009 [8–10]. Harbor facilities in Izu Islands have escape places of inhabitants, transportations of people who are injured, and transport bases of reliefs to the earthquake victims. Airports cover an important role in information assemblages, transportation of injured, and transport of reliefs with heli-ports in Izu Islands. Moreover, it is necessary to execute disaster prevention training, which covers regional trait of each islands constantly. In future, maintenance of harbors being able to berth ferryboat will be required [16]. The Tokyo Metropolitan Government created an itemized checklist for municipalities' officials, in charge of disaster prevention, to be used for tsunami disaster prevention measures, as shown in Table 14 [14]. The signs for tsunami hazard area and the objective point for tsunami evacuation, as shown in Figs. 17 and 18, are prepared and setup in the island. These signs were designed by the Survey Committee for Graphics Symbols for Disaster Preparedness. Municipalities in inland areas use these signs to call public attention to Tsunami and manage evacuations. The signs for Tsunami hazard area are installed at the potential flooded area and for reminder or leading people to the escape target point. The signs of the objective point for Tsunami evacuation are installed at the nonpotential flooded area, for clear indication of the escape target point and for the attention to escape to the higher area [14].

Being prepared for possible tsunamis each municipality creates tsunami hazard maps. Figure 19 shows an example of hazard maps at the Niijima Harbor. The inundation water depth is −2.0 to −0.5 m at the coastline, and −0.5 m at the area a bit away form the coast.

The tsunami warning is using the siren for the evacuation from tsunami hazards. There are four kinds of siren warning: (1) major Tsunami warning is audible for 3 s and stops for 2 s intervals, (2) tsunami warning is audible for 5 s and stops for 6 s, (3) tsunami advisory is audible for 10 s and stops for 2 s, and (4) tsunami advisory and Tsunami warning canceled is audible for 10 s, stops for 2 s, and then audible for 1 min. Also, the disaster message dial is used in the case when the telephone is dead during disaster. The telephone number of disaster message is 171 in Japan. The disaster Radio Broadcast is broadcast live for residents about the scale of tsunami: "alert closely because the tsunami 3 m above at high ground will

Table 14: The checklist of tsunami measures.

Item	Points
Information of earthquake tsunami	Understand the past earthquake tsunami.
Information of inundation areas	Confirm the arrival time of tsunami and the magnitude of earthquake.
	Consider measures of tsunami disaster reduction.
Refuge measures	Confirm the refuge measures by tsunami disaster drill.
	Act on the basis of the refuge on foot.
	Prohibit the usage of car.
	Inform widely the resident by the hazard map and tsunami disaster drill.
Notification of tsunami warning	Confirm preparations of communication throughout tsunami disaster drill.
	Inform widely the resident by communicating with the public relations magazine, hazard-map, siren, broadcasting, publicity car, house radio, etc.
	Inform widely the means of communication throughout the tsunami disaster drill.
	Introduce the automatic starting system of disaster public radio to inform certainly and quickly for the resident.
	Arrange the refuge system of communicating the sea change by the occurrence of tsunami.
Hazard symbol and guide signs	Place the hazard symbol and guide signs at the forecasting inundation area and the target point of refuge.
	Place symbols and signs in the order of priority based on the plan.
	Inform the place of hazard symbols and guide signs to the resident by hazard maps, public papers and tsunami disaster drill.
Evacuation route	Set the evacuation route to the place of refuge in information of tsunami hazard map.
	Maintenance of evacuation route.
Emergency stair	Set the emergency stair at the necessary place.
	Inform the place of emergency stair to the resident.
	Maintenance of emergency stair.
Refuge	Check location and accommodation of refuge.
	Keep up the bare necessities of refuge (lighting, lavatory, water supply, telephone, small car, etc.)
	Stockpile water and food.
	Place sign and guide of refuge.
	Inform the location of refuge for the resident throughout the public newspaper and the hazard map.

Continued

Table 14: *Continued*

Item	Points
Cooperation with community	Grasp people who need assistant for tsunami. Make preparations to support and help people who need assistant. Enforce the cooperation with community. Make and enforce the voluntary organization for disaster prevention. Inform the necessity of cooperation with community for the resident throughout tsunami disaster drill.
Evacuation guidance	Prescribe how to evacuation for residents and visitors. Check the evacuation preparedness throughout tsunami disaster drill.
Preparation of rescue and salvage	Confirm the communication system with Tokyo Metropolitan Government, fire station and police office. Check the emergency power supply.
Preparation of rescue and salvage	Confirm the conveyance preparation of patients to the outside of islands by cooperation of government, fire fighting, police, and self-defense force. Confirm the preparation of rescue and salvage throughout tsunami disaster drill.
Measures for customer coastal	Measures for evacuation behavior of surfers, swimmers, fishing visitors, divers, etc. (advance notice of precautionary warning: siren and handbill). Guide and train for lifeguards.
Measures for fishermen	Set the means of escape for fishermen on land, beach and ship.
Wireless station for disaster prevention	Make the installation diagram. Keep the out of place and set as the need arises. Check the status hearing. Master the operation.
Tsunami disaster facility	Put the tsunami warehouse in good condition. (store food, medical supplies, etc.)
Accommodation suppliers	Guide the evacuation guidance of visitors for the accommodation supplies. Open the meeting of tsunami disaster for accommodation supplies. Prepare the hazard map in the accommodation.
Earthquake emergency plan	Keep the law and the target entities. Guide the planning.
Lifeline	Confirm the recovery framework. Set the emergency water supplies.
Road	Check the traffic control in evacuation time. Secure the bypass in flooded area. Secure the emergency vehicles priority road.

Item	Points
Measures of isolated area	Keep the estimated isolated area by tsunami disaster. Confirm the communication means and put isolated area in good condition if necessary. Confirm the recovery framework for road administrators. Confirm the aid system for the estimated isolated area.
Information for the resident	Take public relations for tsunami (publicity papers and hazard map). Carry out the disaster management course and training education of disaster leaders. Apply the record of tsunami in the past. Consider the education of tsunami at school. Carry out the tsunami emergency drill periodically.

Figure 17: Sign of the Tsunami hazard area.

Figure 18: Sign of the escape target point from Tsunami.

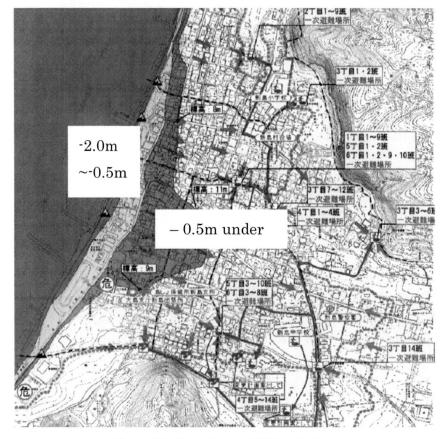

Figure 19: Hazard map of Niijima harbor.

be forecasted" in the case of major Tsunami warning, "alert because the tsunami 2 m at high ground will be forecasted" in the case of Tsunami warning, and "alert because the tsunami 0.5 m at high ground will be forecasted" in the case of tsunami warning note. Tsunami is informed to residents through the official report and public relations as follows: (1) security is the greatest enemy if the earthquake shock is too little or not; (2) do not use cars to evacuate to higher ground rather than ground remote from the cost; (3) inform family and neighbors, and evacuate at high grounds when Tsunami warning or Tsunami advisory are issued, and do not return until the Tsunami warning is canceled; (4) notice at high tide because the water level will be high; (5) do not enter immediate area of coasts and rivers until the Tsunami warning or Tsunami advisory is canceled; (6) evacuate at once when the tsunami warning or the tsunami warning advisory is warned because the velocity of tsunami is very fast; (7) evacuate until the sea surface becomes calm because tsunami often recurs; (8) take care of the low tides; (9) listen a sound information by radio, television, disaster radio broadcast, etc.; (10) discuss about the evacuation site with family in advance.

7 Conclusions

At first, it will be considered that the appropriate human population exists on each island, that is, the human population of Izu Islands is well established. It is an example that the human energy of Izu Islands has been rising year after year against a decline in population every year as shown in Tables 1, 11 and 12. There is a limit of the numbers evacuating from Izu Islands to other places in a state of emergency such as volcanic eruption or Tsunami.

Secondly, maintaining essential infrastructure to be used in emergencies is important. The investment extending over a long period of time is required for conservation of Izu Islands. Because of this, various plans like 10-year (2003–2012) plan for the promotion of isolated islands in Tokyo have been formulated by the Tokyo Metropolitan Government, and the important policy is cooperated with agriculture and fishery, tourism, total transport network, information dispatch function, and disaster prevention.

Finally, disaster prevention measures need to be communicated to all island inhabitants. The improvement of the following facilities and equipments are being promoted so that disaster management activities can be conducted quickly and smoothly: observation equipment such as meteorological satellites, weather observation radar, and seismometers; materials and machinery required for emergency response such as firefighting equipment, water tanks, and power generators; systems for liaising and communicating emergency information such as telecommunications or broadcasting facilities; transportation vehicles such as helicopters, ships, and automobiles; facilities for evacuation and headquarters for disaster countermeasures. In addition, projects such as fireproofing buildings, providing evacuation routes, areas, and facilities for disaster preparation bases have been carried out.

References

[1] http://law.e-gov.go.jp/htm|data//s28/s28HO072.html, *The Law for Development of Isolated Islands*, Japanese Government, 2002.

[2] http://en.wikipedia.org/wiki/Izu-islands, *Izu islands*, Wikipedia, the free encyclopedia.

[3] Tokyo Metropolitan Government, *The Promotion Plan of Isolated Island in Tokyo*, 2004.

[4] Foundation of Tokyo Metropolitan Government and Communication of Islands, *The Public Cooperation of Promotion in Izu and Ogasawara Islands*, 1998.

[5] Tokyo Metropolitan Government, *TOKYO Handy Guide*, 2010.

[6] Japanese Government, *Population Census*, 2006.

[7] Tokyo Metropolitan Government, *Land use in Tokyo*, 2009.

[8] Tokyo Metropolitan Government, *Outline of Ohshima Subprefecture*, 2009.

[9] Tokyo Metropolitan Government, *Outline of Miyake Subprefecture*, 2009.

[10] Tokyo Metropolitan Government, *Outline of Hachijou Subprefecture*, 2009.

[11] Tokyo Metropolitan Government, Bureau of Harbor, *Outline of Projects in 2011*, 2011.

[12] Health Center of Isolated Island in Tokyo, *Outline of Social Works*, Tokyo Metropolitan Government, 2008.

[13] Asahi newspaper, *Minryoku (2000–2005)*, Asahi Newspaper Office, 2000–2005.

[14] Tokyo Metropolitan Government, *Tokyo Metropolitan Government Disaster Prevention Homepage*, http://www.bousai.metro.tokyo.jp/english/e-tmg/tsunami.html (lead in 2009).

[15] Tokyo Metropolitan Government, *TMG's Disaster Prevention Information*, http://www.bousai.metro.tpkyo.jp/english/e-tmg/system.htr (lead in 2009).

[16] Tokyo Metropolitan Government, *Business Plan of Earthquake Disaster Measure in the Tokyo Metropolitan Government*, 2004.

CHAPTER 7

Health-related impacts of Tsunami disasters

Mark E. Keim[1,2]

[1]*Senior Science Advisor, Office of Terrorism Preparedness and Emergency Response, National Center of Environmental Health, Agency for Toxic Substances and Disease Registry Centers for Disease Control & Prevention, Atlanta, GA, USA*
[2]*Adjunct Professor Emory University, Rollins School of Public Health, Atlanta, GA, USA*

Abstract

Tsunamis have the potential to cause an enormous impact upon the health of millions of people. During the last half of the twentieth century, more people were killed by tsunamis than by earthquakes [1]. Most recently, a major emergency response operation has been underway in the northeast Japan following a devastating tsunami triggered by the biggest earthquake on record in Japan. This natural disaster has been described as the most expensive in world history [2]. There are few resources in the public health literature that describe the characteristics and epidemiology of tsunami-related disasters, as a whole. This chapter reviews the phenomenology and impact of tsunamis as a significant public health hazard.

1 Background nature of tsunamis

1.1 Definition

The Japanese word tsunami translates in English to "harbor wave."

A tsunami is a series of ocean waves generated by any disturbance that displaces a large water mass [3]. About 90–95% of tsunamis are caused by large earthquakes (usually Richter magnitude 6.5 or greater); the remainders are primarily due to volcanic eruptions (like the eruption of Mt. Krakatau in 1883) or landslides (like the 1998 Papua New Guinea tsunami generated by a submarine landslide). There are also composite events such as the 1946 subduction earthquake in the Aleutian Islands that triggered a landslide-generated tsunami killing

159 people in Hawaii [4]. Prehistoric geological evidence has also implicated meteorites or comet impacts as a rare cause of tsunami (the most notable is located near the Yucatán Peninsula in the Gulf of Mexico) [5].

To understand tsunamis, it is helpful to distinguish them from wind-generated waves or tides. Wind blowing across the ocean deforms the surface into relatively short waves to create currents restricted to a shallow surface layer. Strong gales are able to whip up waves 100 ft, (30 m), or higher in the open ocean but even these do not move deep water [6]. Wind-generated surface waves typically have a high frequency and short wavelength (distance between wave crests) as compared to the extremely low frequency and long wavelength of tsunami waves. Tsunamis often are called by the popular name, "tidal waves," but this is a misnomer. They are not caused by the tidal action of the moon and sun like the regular ocean tides. Rather they are long water waves generated by sudden displacement of the earth under water.

1.2 Causes of tsunamis

The type of earthquake is as important as its strength in determining whether or not a tsunami will occur. The earth's crust is made up of a "jigsaw puzzle" of tectonic plates that abut and move against each other. Subduction zones are faults in the earth's crust in which one tectonic plate overrides another. Movement along this type of fault typically produces the vertical land movement necessary to generate a tsunami. Subduction earthquakes can impart a vertical displacement on the earth's surface that is hundreds of miles long and thus displace billions of tons of water. Earthquakes that produce largely horizontal movement (i.e., the San Andreas Fault in California, US) do not typically generate tsunamis. In addition, the causative earthquake must occur at relatively shallow, (<31 miles or 50 km), depths underground in order to efficiently transfer ground energy to the water above. Great trans-ocean tsunamis are typically caused by massive subduction earthquakes whose rupture zones extend several hundreds of kilometers along the trench. These earthquake-generated tsunamis spread outwards in all directions from the point of origin [7]. In comparison, tsunamis triggered by submarine landslides produce a relatively narrow radiation pattern resulting in a focused beam of energy with the potential of also reaching far afield [4].

Giant submarine landslides (and impacts from extra-terrestrial sources such as comets and meteors) have the potential to create extremely large waves referred to as mega-tsunamis. At least 100 mega-tsunamis in different parts of the world have been recorded in the past 2000 years according to interpretation of the sedimentologic and geomorphic imprints left by these events [8]. Mega-tsunamis produced by giant submarine landslides were first proposed for Hawaii and have since been implicated globally on other oceanic islands along with continental margins [9]. For instance, marine deposits in the Hawaiian Islands that lie up to 1230 ft (375 m) above the sea level on the island of Lanai have been attributed to the action of a mega-tsunami-generated by giant submarine landslides from Mauna Loa volcano on the big island of Hawaii [10]. Giant wave deposits found in the Bahamas coincide with a prehistoric volcano collapse in La Palma, Canary Islands [11].

1.3 The physics of tsunami phenomenon

Regardless of their origin, tsunamis evolve through the three overlapping but quite distinct physical processes: generation by any force that disturbs the water column, propagation from deeper water near the source to shallow coastal areas, and, finally, inundation of the dry land.

Generation is the process by which a seafloor disturbance, such as movement along a fault, reshapes the sea surface into a tsunami. Vertical displacement of the ocean floor results in a transfer of seismic energy to the entire column of water above. Propagation of the tsunami transports seismic energy away from the earthquake site through the water just as shaking moves the energy through the earth during an earthquake. Once the tsunami is generated, a series of extremely low frequency, long wavelength, (~186 miles or 300 km), waves are propagated in an expanding radius from the area of displacement traveling at a speed proportional to the square root of the depth of water reaching up to 600 miles (965 km) per hour in the deep ocean.

Because the energy is spread throughout such a large volume in deep water and have such a long wavelength between crests, tsunamis may be only a few feet (<1 m) high in the mid ocean, making them capable of passing under ocean-going ships with little disturbance or detection. The physical dynamics of the fluid pressure wave allow it to travel great distances with very little loss of energy. For example, a subduction earthquake occurring on January 26, 1700 at the Cascadia subduction zone encompassing western Washington and Oregon generated a tsunami that destroyed the island of Honshu, Japan [12, 13].

The dependence of wave speed on water depth also causes individual waves to slow down as they approach shallow water, so they begin to overtake one another decreasing the distance between them in a process called shoaling. Refraction of the wave off the seafloor and shoaling focuses the same amount of energy into a smaller volume of water creating higher waves and faster currents as the tsunami reaches land [6].

The last stage is inundation in which a tsunami may run ashore as a breaking wave, a wall of water or a tide-like flood is perhaps most difficult to model. Vertical run-up typically takes only 2–3 m to cause damage along the shoreline. Horizontal inundation, if unimpeded by coastal cliffs or other steep typography, can penetrate hundreds perhaps even thousands of meters inland.

Vertical run-up of a tsunami is usually 10–50 ft (3–15 m) high. Wave heights averaged 80 ft (24 m) above the sea level along the western coastline of Sumatra during inundation of the 2004 Indian Ocean tsunami earthquake [14]. A 230 ft (70 m) wave was recorded following the 1964 Alaska earthquake [15]. Extremely rare mega-tsunamis produced by giant submarine landslides have been implicated globally [9]. The highest mega-tsunami wave ever witnessed occurred at Lituya Bay, Alaska in 1950. It was triggered by an 8.0 magnitude earthquake-induced landslide and reached the height of 1720 ft (524 m) above the shoreline, (three stories higher than the former World Trade Center of New York City) [3].

As the tsunami enters shallow water near coastlines, the kinetic energy previously spread throughout the large volume of ocean deep ocean water becomes concentrated to a much smaller volume of water, resulting in a tremendous destructive potential as it inundates the land. Successive crests may arrive to shore at period intervals of every 10–45 min. This phenomenon is particularly problematic when responders attempt to rescue victims from the water after the first wave, only to become victimized by subsequent waves themselves. A single tsunami event may comprise up to 12 wave crests. Prior to inundation of the wave crest, the sea often appears to recede for an unusually far distance.

During 1960, Chilean tsunami that struck Hilo, Hawaii, this phenomenon tended to attract more people to the shoreline and into the ocean itself where they were then caught up in the oncoming wave crest. One village in Papua New Guinea reportedly recognized this as a sign of pending tsunami and took protective actions for shoreline evacuation. In Simelue, Indonesia, an old song about moving to high ground when the earth shakes is reported to have saved lives and resulted in a relatively low death rate compared to neighboring Sumatra (which was farther from the quake epicenter).

2 Scope and relative importance of tsunamis

Tsunamis have occurred in all the oceans and in the Mediterranean Sea. About 90–95% of the world's tsunamis have occurred in the Pacific Ocean due to its relatively large size and its bordering "Ring of Fire" comprised of major tectonic subduction fault zones. Great trans-Pacific tsunamis are typically caused by massive earthquakes located at these subduction zones and occur at an interval of about once a decade [1].

Since 1900, there have been 52 tsunami events worldwide that resulted in at least one fatality [16]. During the 1990s, a total of 82 tsunamis were reported worldwide – a rate much higher than the historical average of 57 per decade (likely a result of better reporting) [6]. During the past decade since 1992, 14 tsunami events have caused over 182,059 deaths, and at least $USD 267 billion in damage [16] (see Table 1).

The 2004 Indian Ocean tsunami alone killed 165,708 people (91% of all tsunami deaths since 1990) and directly affected two million people in 12 nations [16]. WHO has estimated the number of injuries that required treatment as result of the 2004 Indian Ocean tsunami at about 500,000 [17].

In a 100-year period from 1895 to 1995, there were 454 tsunamis recorded in the Pacific Ocean, the deadliest 94 killed over 51,000 people [3]. Over the past Century in Japan, approximately 15% of 150 tsunamis were damaging or fatal. More than half of the 34 tsunamis that struck Indonesia in the past 100 years were damaging or fatal. More than 200 tsunamis are known to have affected the United States since the time of first written records. Total damage is estimated at half $1 billion and 470 casualties, primarily in Alaska and Hawaii [3]. Hawaii, because of its mid-ocean location, is especially vulnerable to such Pacific wide tsunamis. Twelve damaging tsunamis have struck Hawaii since 1895. In the most destructive,

Table 1: Fatal tsunami/earthquake disasters 1992–2011.

Year	Location	Estimated damage ($USD million)	Fatalities
1992	Nicaragua	25	179
1992	Indonesia	100	2500
1993	Japan	1000	239
1994	Indonesia	2.2	239
1994	Philippines	3.7	81
1995	Mexico	21.1	6
1996	Indonesia	1.2	9
1996	Peru	Not available	7
1996	Indonesia	4.2	161
1998	Papua New Guinea	Not available	2182
2004	Indian Ocean	4500	165,708
2009	South Pacific	160	186
2010	Chile	30,000	562
2011	Japan	235,000	21,911 (as of 3/21/11)
1990–2011	Totals	267,820.4	182,059

Source: Centre for Research on the Epidemiology of Disasters [16].

159 people died there in 1946 from killer waves that were generated almost 2300 miles (3700 km) away in Alaska's Aleutian Islands [3].

The Alaska Aleutian subduction zone poses an immediate tsunami threat to the western coast of the United States. Another major tsunami threat is located off the coast of Washington state or Oregon and northern California, known as the Cascadia subduction zone. The probability of a major earthquake occurrence before 2045 is estimated at 35% along this zone. A Cascadia-born tsunami disaster could cost the region between $1.25 and $6.25 billion [6]. A mega-tsunami resulting from the collapse of La Palma, Canary Islands could strike the Caribbean, Florida and the rest of the US eastern seaboard with a vertical run up of 164 ft, (50 m), high and a horizontal inundation of 12 miles (20 km) inland [11].

The human health effects of tsunamis cannot be understated. In addition to the public health and medical consequences of these disasters, the socioeconomic, cultural, and psychological impact of tsunamis have had an enormous and long-lasting impact throughout the world and a direct effect upon human development in general. Total damage and losses after the 2004 Indian Ocean tsunami are estimated at $USD 4.5–7 billion. One hundred seventy four million dollars of those losses were incurred by the health care system with an estimated health sector reconstruction cost in the order of $USD 107 million [17]. The World Bank has estimated that damages due to the 2011 Japan tsunami may range from $USD 122 to 265 billion, (2.5–4% of Japan's GDP) [2].

3 Factors that contribute to the tsunami problem

Despite the remarkable advances in tsunami monitoring and early warning, death tolls remain remarkably high. The high death tolls are partly due to increases in coastal populations and high-risk land use patterns. Settlement patterns increasingly place dense populations in close proximity to the tsunami hazard. In addition, the overwhelming majority of coastal communities located in the tsunami-prone Pacific basin have no direct linkage to the multimillion dollar Tsunami Warning System (TWS).

Most nations at risk lack the resources necessary to effectively warn and evacuate coastal populations. After the Chilean earthquake of 2010, experts have debated how much emergency-response planners should rely on tsunami forecasts [18]. Difficulties in modeling and predicting the vertical run up of tsunamis as they approach the shore also contribute to a degree of uncertainty in advance warning that may affect the public's perception of risk. A false alarm that triggered the evacuation of Honolulu on May 7, 1986, cost Hawaii more than $30 million in lost salaries and business revenues [6]. Even the most reliable warning is ineffective if people do not respond appropriately. Community education is therefore perhaps the most important aspect of any tsunami mitigation program.

4 Factors affecting tsunami occurrence and severity

The effects of the tsunami may vary with factors including: proximity to the earthquake epicenter; physical geography of the region; the force of the waves when they hit the shore; and the extent to which the waves penetrate the shoreline. Proximity to the epicenter of the earthquake or submarine landslide is directly associated with an increased severity due to the amount of seismic energy transferred during vertical run up and horizontal inundation. During 2004 Indian Ocean tsunami, Indonesia (the closest land to the epicenter) suffered the most severe tsunami strikes, followed by Andaman Nicobar, Thailand, Maldives, Sri Lanka, India, and eastern Africa as distance from the epicenter increased.

Refraction by bumps, grooves, and troughs on the seafloor can shift the wave direction, especially as it travels into shallow water. In particular, wave fronts tend to align parallel to the shorelines with a wraparound protruding head land before smashing into it with greatly focused incident energy [6]. The author observed this phenomenon as particularly evident in the total destruction of the cities of Banda Aceh, and Calang, Indonesia where the waves entered and exited the headlands from both sides of the peninsula-like headland. After the 1946, Aleutian Island earthquake vertical run ups in the Marquesas (4660 miles or 7500 km from the source), were larger than in Hawaii (2300 miles or 3700 km closer) due to a funneling effect in narrow valleys [4].

The effects of tsunamis on coastal areas are characterized by the maximum destructive force of the water's edge. Damage farther inland is potentially high even though the force of the wave has diminished because of the floating debris that batters the inland installations. Low-lying coastal areas and coral atolls (such as the Maldives) also suffer an increased severity of destruction.

5 Public health impact: historical perspective

There is strong evidence that a magnitude 8 earthquake generated along the Cascadia fault zone shook the northwest coast of the United States causing a tidal wave that hit the Japanese island of Honshu on January 26, 1700 [12]. It is believed a tsunami killed more than 30,000 people within 75 miles (120 km) of the catastrophic eruption at Krakatau, Indonesia volcano in 1883. Of the 12 most deadly tsunamis during 1900–2011, four occurred in Japan and four were in Indonesia, with all but two originating in the Pacific Ocean. Most resulted in several hundred to several thousand deaths per event [16].

The 1946, Aleutian island tsunami was the most destructive in the history of the Hawaiian Islands. More than 150 persons were killed, while damage to property amounted to $26 million. The United States reacted to this disaster by setting up the Pacific Tsunami Warning Center in Hawaii in 1948 [6].

Earthquake-triggered landslides have the potential to create tsunamis much larger than expected for the size of the earthquake. In 1998, the Papua New Guinea tsunami generated waves up to 50 ft (15 m) high, killing 2200 people after a magnitude 7.1 earthquake. Two rare landslides in the western Atlantic also fuel the tsunami concern in the eastern United states. In 1929, an earthquake-triggered landslide off Newfoundland's grand Banks generated a tsunami that killed 51 people [19].

The single largest tsunami disaster in recorded history occurred in the Indian Ocean on December 26, 2004 along the Andaman Nicobar fault zone. The tsunami killed more than 300,000 people and displaced 2 million persons in 12 nations. Most recently, a powerful 9.0-magnitude earthquake hit Japan on March 11, 2011, unleashing massive tsunami waves that resulted in widespread damage and destruction. According to the Government of Japan as of March 21, at least 21,911 were dead and missing and 2644 injured [20].

6 Factors influencing mortality and morbidity

6.1 Mortality trends

The vast majority of tsunami-related deaths occur immediately [1]. In a large tsunami, deaths frequently exceed the number of injured [1, 21]. The number of tsunami-related deaths exceeded the number of injuries caused by the 2011 Japan tsunami by a ratio of nearly 7:1 [20]. The vast majority of those causalities were sustained as a result of the tsunami rather than the earthquake. Average death rates are believed to be 50% for the population affected by tsunami [1]. The 30,000 inhabitants of Calang in Aceh province, Indonesia suffered an estimated 70% mortality rate during inundation of the December 26, 2004, tsunami [22].

Most tsunami deaths ultimately result from drowning. However, the tsunami does not consist only of water. It also contains a great amount of very heavy debris traveling with tremendous momentum. The 2004 Indian Ocean tsunami (and associated debris) was estimated to have travelled at 30 miles per hour, (48 km/h), when on shore in Aceh province, Indonesia.

Deaths from tsunami injuries occur in three phases. Victims usually succumb to injuries that are incompatible with life (drowning, severe head, chest, and spine injuries) within the first few minutes. Then immediate complications set in over the next few minutes to hours (such as bleeding, lung collapse, and blood clots in the lung). Finally, these immediate causes of death are followed by delayed complications over the coming days that are mostly associated with infectious disease (such as wound infections and aspiration pneumonia) [23, 24].

According to a survey recently carried out by Oxfam, four times as many women than men were killed in the tsunami-affected areas of Indonesia, Sri Lanka, and India [25]. One study of disaster-related mortality in Sri Lanka observed a higher mortality rate among females, children and the elderly. Other risk factors included: being indoors at the time of the tsunami; the degree of house destruction; and fishing as an occupation [26].

6.2 Tsunami-associated illness and injury

A tsunami directly injures the victims by the mechanism of blunt trauma and penetrating injury [26]. People are bludgeoned by concrete slabs and felled trees, stabbed by jagged sheets of metal and glass, tangled up in manacles of wire, and impaled onto tree limbs and bamboo. Soil, small pieces of wood, glass, and metal in the contaminated saltwater penetrate the soft tissues of the body at high velocity. The predominant pattern of injury comprised multiple large-scale soft tissue wounds of lower extremities and open fractures [26]. Wound contamination was also a major clinical problem [24].

When the 2004 Indian Ocean tsunami hit the western coast of southern Thailand, 6 to 8 huge waves with a height of 15–22 ft (5–7 m) destroyed almost everything along the beach and inundated areas more than 984 ft (300 m) from the seashore. Most of the survivors had minimal to moderate injuries to the body and extremities [27].

No survivor of the Papua New Guinea tsunami was found to have head, spine, thorax, or abdomen injuries, implying that survival of these life-threatening injuries was virtually impossible in that remote setting with delayed resuscitative and surgical care [26]. Bone fractures, soft tissue injuries, and near-drowning were the most common conditions reported among survivors in both the Papua New Guinea and the Indian Ocean tsunamis [27–30].

6.3 Infectious diseases

The role of active case finding and generous availability of health services surely played a role in the noted eight-fold increase of acute respiratory infections in

Aceh province, but it can generally be agreed that acute respiratory infection did increase substantially following the 2004 tsunami. Cases of acute respiratory infections decreased significantly after the first 5 weeks suggesting that the largest caseload occurs within a month after the disaster event, and is related to tsunami-induced near-drowning as a major causative factor [31].

Near-drowning is common in tsunamis and is frequently associated with aspiration pneumonia or "tsunami lung," a necrotizing pneumonia notable for flora commonly associated with sea water near drowning (e.g. *Aeromonas* and *Pseudomonas* species). However, after the Indian Ocean tsunami, cultures from the upper respiratory tract specimens also grew an unusually high rate of relatively uncommon pathogens that are not associated with sea water aspiration (such as multiple-resistant *Acinetobacter baumanii*, methicillin-resistant *Staphylococcus aureus*, *Stenotrophomonas maltophilia*, *Burkholderia pseudomallei*, and Candida albicans) [24, 28, 32].

After the 2011 Japanese, tsunami physicians reported a combined pulmonary infection of the Legionella and multiple antibiotic resistant *Escherichia coli* [33]. There were also other case reports of tsunami lung associated with multiple uncommon pathogens (including *Stenotrophus maltophilia, Legionaella pneumophilia, Burkholderia cepacia, and Pseudomonas aeruginosa*) [34]. There was also a case of pleural empyema reportedly associated with the patient's aspiration of a small pine tree branch [35]. One patient that survived near-drowning was diagnosed with *E. coli* pneumonia in combination with a fungal sinusitis and meningitis [36].

In addition to the aspiration pneumonia described as "tsunami lung," the rate of hospitalizations for infectious disease doubled during the one month following after the 2011 Japan tsunami as compared to the same period during 2010. Community-acquired pneumonia (caused by *Streptococcus pneumoniae, Moraxella catarrhalis, and Haemophilus influenza*) comprised 43% of those hospital admissions for infectious disease during that period [37].

Melioidosis, a serious infection caused by *B. pseudomallei*, is reported most commonly in Southeast Asia and northern Australia. The infection is acquired by contamination of breaks in the skin or by inhalation. Several cohorts of patients in southeast Thailand and the Phuket area was diagnosed with melioidosis after aspiration related to the Indian Ocean tsunami. Immunocompromise was an associated risk factor as would be expected [23, 38, 39].

Tsunami wounds are inevitably contaminated with soil, debris, and foreign bodies. Wound infections were common after the 2004 Indian Ocean tsunami and comprised 16.9% of all diagnoses by January 10 at the International Committee of the Red Cross (ICRC) field hospital in Calang, Indonesia) [22] and 15% of all consultations at the ICRC field hospital in Banda Aceh [31]. Subcutaneous tissue infection comprised 12% of hospital admissions for infectious disease during the month following the 2011 Japan tsunami [37].

Similar to acute respiratory infections, wound infections also frequently involved multiple, relatively uncommon pathogens (such as *P. Aeruginosa, Stenotrophomonas maltophilia,* and *Klebsiella pneumonia*) [24, 30, 40]. Acute open marine trauma is not infrequently associated with subsequent infection [24]. However cultures also indicated significant coexistent contamination with highly resistant species uncommon to aquatic surroundings (such as multiple-resistant *A. baumannii*, extended-spectrum beta lactamase producing *E. coli*, methicillin-resistant *Staphylococcus aureus* and *Candida* species). One case report described multifocal cutaneous mucormycosis complicating polymicrobial wound infections in a tsunami survivor from Sri Lanka [40].

As was also the case in populations affected by hurricanes Andrew and Iniki, tetanus cases increased after the 2004 Indian Ocean tsunami and 2011 Japanese tsunami as result of soil-contaminated injuries sustained at the time of impact [31, 37]. The number of cases then returned to the baseline within 1 month of the event, signifying that all cases were the result of wound contamination sustained during the tsunami event itself [31].

The correct identification of pathogens and their antimicrobial susceptibility is essential to reduce mortality, especially in the case of wound infections and unusual respiratory infections after tsunami. Therefore, sufficient diagnostic and confirmation capacities such as radiology and laboratory services should be made available. For this reason, emergency medical teams should be aware of resistance patterns in the target areas before or shortly after arrival to respond appropriately to the situation. Emergency health kits should include medications that offer appropriate broad-spectrum antimicrobial coverage for such infections as those that would be expected after tsunami.

Contrary to initial concerns for outbreaks of malaria, measles, cholera, and dengue, [41–46], the Indian Ocean tsunami (like the overwhelming majority of all previous seismic disasters) was not associated with epidemics of infectious disease [31].

Despite reports of a significant risk of vector abundance with enhanced transmission potential [45] no increases in cases for malaria or dengue were noted in any nation of the tsunami-affected regions of Southeast Asia [31] Ironically, the post-tsunami monthly incidence of malaria in Aceh province, Indonesia was more than 10 times lower than the comparable monthly rate over the last five years prior to the 2004 tsunami [31]. Experience has shown that these diseases, however commonly believed, are not always a priority immediately after any natural disaster [31].

6.4 Worsening of chronic diseases

As is the case with most disasters, tsunamis have been reported to also exacerbate pre-existing chronic diseases among the population. After the Japan tsunami, the number of patients with acute decompensated heart failure nearly doubled as compared to the predisaster. This impact was found to peak at 3 to 4 weeks after the disaster. It is thought to be associated with stress, sudden changes in activities of daily life, diet and disruption of availability of prescribed medications [47]. Other studies revealed poor management of diabetes and hypertension among patients that were displaced by the tsunami (presumably many of the same reasons as for the heart failure) [48, 49]. One report described a high prevalence of deep vein thrombosis in disaster shelters were set up in flooded areas after the tsunami. This was largely attributed to inactivity, as well as dehydration, and gastrointestinal illness brought on by inadequate water and sanitation in these shelters [50]. The incidence of peptic ulcers was 1.5-fold increased, and in particular, the incidence of hemorrhagic ulcers was 2.2-fold increased [51].

6.5 Psychosocial consequences

Behavioral health effects are among the most chronic and debilitating outcomes of natural disasters, including tsunamis [52, 53]. Clinical symptoms of posttraumatic psychological stress response have been widely noted among tsunami survivors and relatives [24].

Among survivors of the tsunami in southern Thailand, elevated rates of symptoms of posttraumatic stress disorder (PTSD), anxiety, and depression among adults were reported 8 weeks after the disaster with higher rates for anxiety and depression than PTSD symptoms. Nine months after the disaster, the rates of those reporting the symptoms decreased but were still elevated [54].

Prevalence of PTSD symptoms among children in displacement camps of southern Thailand were elevated as compared to nonaffected villages. After 9 months, the prevalence of PTSD symptoms among children's and camps had not significantly decreased [55].

The monumental devastation of the December 2004 Indian Ocean tsunami also prompted a meta-analysis of the psychosocial consequences of natural disasters in developing countries versus developed countries. A much higher proportion of the population in developing nations sustained severe loss and extreme trauma and experiences that constitute clinically significant distress as compared to developed nations (for not only tsunamis, but all natural disasters in general) [53, 56]. Posttraumatic stress and psychological changes were reported to increase along with stress-related hormones among populations affected by the Japan tsunami and earthquake [57]. This was also exacerbated by the potential for radiological exposure due to the Fukushima nuclear incident. High levels of anxiety distress and anger were noted among British nationals in Japan following the Fukushima nuclear accident [58]. As a result of concerns for potential radioactive contamination among international travelers, some governments established screening protocols for detection of external radioactive material contamination at points of entry. Despite resource intensive screening, only 3 out of 543,000 travelers screened were found to have measurable contamination [59].

7 Conclusion

Tsunamis represent a significant public health hazard for coastal populations located near tectonic subduction zones. The public health impacts of tsunamis are well known and predictable. The overwhelmingly most significant health impact is that of mass fatalities due to drowning. Other health impacts are related to traumatic injuries, unusual respiratory and skin infections, disruption of the public health infrastructure, worsening of chronic diseases, population displacement, and psychological stress.

Disclaimer

The material in this chapter reflects solely the views of the author. It does not necessarily reflect the policies or recommendations of the Centers for Disease Control and Prevention or the US Department of Health and Human Services.

References

[1] McCarty, D., Tsunamis. *Disaster Medicine*, eds. D. Hogan & J. Burstein, Philadelphia, PA: Lippincott, William and Wilkins; New York, NY, pp. 229–234, 2002.

[2] World Bank. The recent earthquake and tsunami in Japan: implications for East Asia. World Bank East Asia and Pacific Economic Update 2011, vol. 1. Available at http://siteresources.worldbank.org/INTEAPHALFYEARLYUP-DATE/Resources/550192-1300567391916/EAP_Update_March2011_japan.pdf?cid=EXTEAPMonth1 (accessed 22 March 2011).

[3] Boyarsky, I. & Shneiderman, A., Natural and hybrid disasters – causes, effects and management. *Topics in Emergency Medicine*, **24(3)**, pp. 1–25, 2002.

[4] Fryer, G., Watts, P. & Pratson, L., Source of the great tsunami of 1 April 1946: a landslide in the upper Aleutian forearc. *Marine Geology*, **204**, pp. 201–218, 2003.

[5] Bolt, B.A., *Earthquakes: a Primer*. WH Freeman: San Francisco, 1978.

[6] Gonzalez, F., Tsunami. *Scientific American*, **280(5)**, pp. 57–65, 1999.

[7] Perez, E. & Thompson, P., Natural hazards: causes and effects. *Prehospital and Disaster Medicine*, **10(1)**, pp. 66–70, 2005.

[8] Scheffers, A. & Kelletat, D., Sedimentologic and geomorphologic tsunami imprints worldwide – a review. *Earth Science Review*, **63(1–2)**, pp. 83–92, 2003.

[9] McMurtry, G., Watts, P., Fryer, G., Smith, J. & Imamura, F., Giant landslides, mega-tsunamis and paleo-sea level in the Hawaiian Islands. *Marine Geology*, **203**, pp. 219–233, 2004.

[10] Moore, J.G. & Moore, G.W., Deposit from a giant wave on the island of Lanai, Hawaii. *Science*, **226**, pp. 1312–1315, 1984.

[11] Marshall, T., The drowning wave. *New scientist*, **2259**, pp. 26–31, 7 October 2000.

[12] Anonymous. Linking trees to tsunamis. *Science*, **278**, p. 1021, 7 November 1997.

[13] Satake, K., Wang, K. & Atwater, B., Fault slip and seismic moment of the 1700 Cascadia earthquake inferred from Japanese tsunami descriptions. *Journal of Geophysical Research*, 2003.

[14] Paulson, T., New findings super-size our tsunami threat. *Seattle Post Intelligence*. 7 February 2005. Available at http://seattlepi.nwsource.com/local/211012_tsunamiscience07.html (accessed 22 March 2011).

[15] Alaska Division of Emergency Services. *Tsunami! The Great Waves in Alaska*. Alaska Division of Emergency Services: Anchorage, AK, 1992.

[16] Centre for Research on the Epidemiology of Disasters (CRED). *EM-DAT, the International Disaster Database*, 2011. Available at http://www.emdat.be/result-disaster-profiles?disgroup=natural&period=1900%242011&dis_type=Earthquake+%28seismic+activity%29&Submit=Display+Disaster+Profile (accessed 22 March 2011).

[17] Carballo, M., Daita, S. & Hernandez, M., Impact of the tsunami on healthcare systems. *Journal of the Royal Society of Medicine*, **98**, pp. 390–395, 2005.

[18] Schiermeier, Q., Model response to Chile quake? *Nature*, **464(7285)**, pp. 14–5, 2010

[19] Simpson, S. Killer waves on the East Coast? *Scientific American*, **283(4)**, pp. 16–17, 2000.

[20] United Nations Office for the Coordination of Humanitarian Affairs (OCHA). *Japan Earthquake & Tsunami*, Situation report No. 10. 2011, available at http://www.reliefweb.int/rw/rwb.nsf/db900sid/SMDL-8F6DN8?OpenDocument&emid=EQ-2011-000028-JPN (accessed 22 March 2011).

[21] Calder, J. & Mannion, S., Orthopedics in Sri Lanka post-tsunami. *Journal of Bone and Joint Surgery*, **87-B(6)**, pp. 759–761, 2005.

[22] Brennan, R. & Rimba, K., Rapid health assessment in Aceh Jaya District, Indonesia, following the December 26 tsunami. *Emergency Medicine Australasia*, **17**, pp. 341–350, 2005.

[23] Kongsaengdao, S. Treatment of Survivors after the tsunami. *New England Journal of Medicine*, **25(352)**, pp. 2654–2655, 2005.

[24] Maegele, M., Gregor, S. & Steinhausen, E., The long-distance tertiary air transfer and care of tsunami victims: injury pattern and microbial and psychological aspects. *Critical Care Medicine*, **33(5)**, pp. 1143–1144, 2005.

[25] Oxfam International. *The Tsunami's Impact on Women*. Oxfam briefing notes. 2005, available at http://publications.oxfam.org.uk/display.asp?k=002P0179&keyword=tsunami+impact+on+women&sort=SORT_DATE%2Fd&m=2&dc=2 (accessed 22 March 2011.

[26] Nishikiori, N., Abe, T., Costa, D.G., Dharmaratne, S.D., Kunii, O. & Moji, K., Who died as a result of the tsunami? Risk factors of mortality among internally displaced persons in Sri Lanka: a retrospective cohort analysis. *BMC Public Health*, **6**, p. 73, 2006.

[27] Taylor, P., Emonson, D. & Schlimmer, J., Operation Shaddock-the Australian Defence Force response to the tsunami disaster in Papua New Guinea. *Medical Journal of Australia*, **169**, pp. 602–606, 1998.

[28] Watcharong, C., Chuckpaiwong, B. & Mahaisavariya, B., Orthopaedic trauma following tsunami: experience from Phang Nga, Thailand. *Journal of Orthopaedic Surgery*, **13(1)**, pp. 1–2, 2005.

[29] Holian, A. & Keith, P., Orthopedic surgery after Aitape tsunami. *Medical Journal of Australia*, **169**, pp. 606–609, 1998.

[30] Lim, P., Wound infections in tsunami survivors. *Annals of the Academy of Medicine, Singapore*, **34(9)**, pp. 582–585, 2005.

[31] Guha-Sapir, D. & van Panhuis, W., *The Andaman Nicobar Earthquake and Tsunami 2004: Impact on Diseases in Indonesia*. Brussels, Belgium: Centre for Research on the Epidemiology of Disasters, 2005.

[32] Allworth, A., Tsunami lung: a necrotizing pneumonia in survivors of the Asian tsunami. *Medical Journal of Australia*, **182(7)**, p. 364, 2005.

[33] Ebisawa, K., Yamada, N., Okada, S., Suzuki, Y., Satoh, A., Kobayashi, M. & Morikawa, N., Combined Legionella and Escherichia coli lung infection after a tsunami disaster. *Internal Medicine*, **50(19)**, pp. 2233-6, 2011.

[34] Inoue, Y., Fujino, Y., Onodera, M., Kikuchi, S., Shozushima, T., Ogino, N., Mori, K., Oikawa, H., Koeda, Y., Ueda, H., Takahashi, T., Terui, K., Nakadate, T., Aoki, H. & Endo, S., Tsunami lung. *Journal of Anesthesia*, **26(2)**, pp. 246–249, 2012.

[35] Ota, H. & Kawai, H., An unusual case of pleural empyema in a tsunami survivor. *Asian Cardiovascular and Thoracic Annals*, **20(3)**, pp. 344–346, 2012.

[36] Igusa, R., Narumi, S., Murakami, K., Kitawaki, Y., Tamii, T., Kato, M., Sato, M., Tsuboi, M. & Ota, K., Escherichia coli pneumonia in combination with fungal sinusitis and meningitis in a tsunami survivor after the Great East Japan Earthquake. *The Tohoku Journal of Experimental Medicine*, **227(3)**, pp. 179–184, 2012.

[37] Aoyagi, T., Yamada, M., Kunishima, H., Tokuda, K., Yano, H., Ishibashi, N., Hatta, M., Endo, S., Arai, K., Inomata, S., Gu, Y., Kanamori, H., Kitagawa, M., Hirakata, Y. & Kaku, M., Characteristics of infectious diseases in hospitalized patients during the early phase after the 2011 Great East Japan earthquake: pneumonia as a significant reason for hospital care. *Chest*, **143(2)**, pp. 349–356, 2013

[38] Chierakul, W., Winothai, W., Wattanawaitunechai, C., Wuthiekanun, V., Rugtaengan, T., Rattanalertnavee, J., Jitpratoom, P., Chaowagul, W., Singhasivanon, P., White, N.J., Day, N.P. & Peacock, S.J., Melioidososis in six tsunami survivors in Thailand. *Clinical Infectious Diseases*, **41**, pp. 982–990, 2005.

[39] Kateruttanakul, P., Paovilai, W. & Kongsaengdao, S., Respiratory complication of tsunami victims in Phuket and Phang-Nga. *Journal of the Medical Association of Thailand*, **88(6)**, pp. 754–758, 2005.

[40] Andresen, D., Donaldson, A., Choo, L., Knox, A., Klaassen, M., Ursic, C., Vonthethoff, L., Krilis, S. & Konecny, P., Multifocal cutaneous mucormycosis complicating polymicrobial wound infections in a tsunami survivor from Sri Lanka. *Lancet*, **365**, pp. 876–878, 2005.

[41] Moszynski, P., Disease threatens millions in wake of tsunami. *British Medical Journal*, **330**, p. 59, 2005.

[42] Krishnamoorthy, K., Jambulingam, P., Natajaran, R., Shriram, A.N., Das, P.K. & Sehgal, S.C., Altered environment and risk of malaria outbreak in

South Andaman, Andaman & Nicobar islands, India affected as by tsunami. *Malaria Journal*, **4**, p. 32, 2005.

[43] Orellana, C., Tackling infectious disease in the tsunami's wake. *Lancet*, **5**, p. 73, 2005.

[44] Anonymous. WHO appeals for 60 million US dollars to prevent disease outbreaks in tsunami affected Southeast Asia. *Annals of Saudi Medicine*, **25(2)**, p. 178, 2005.

[45] Balaraman, K., Sabesan, S., Jambulingam, P., Gunasekaran, K. & Boopathi Doss, P.S., Risk of outbreak of vector borne diseases in the tsunami hit areas of southern India. *Lancet*, **5**, pp. 128–129, 2005.

[46] Gunasekaran, K., Jamulingam, P., Srinivasan, R., Sadanandane, C., Doss, P.B., Sabesan, S., Balaraman, K. & Das, P., Malaria receptivity in these tsunami hit coastal villages of southern India. *Lancet*, **5**, pp. 531–532, 2005.

[47] Nakamura, M., Tanaka, F., Nakajima, S., Honma, M., Sakai, T., Kawakami, M., Endo, H., Onodera, M., Niiyama, M., Komatsu, T., Sakamaki, K., Onoda, T., Sakata, K., Morino, Y., Takahashi, T. & Makita, S., Comparison of the incidence of acute decompensated heart failure before and after the major tsunami in northeast Japan. *American Journal of Cardiology*, **110(12)**, pp. 1856–1860, 2012.

[48] Kishimoto, M. & Noda, M., The Great East Japan Earthquake: experiences and suggestions for survivors with diabetes (perspective). *PLoS Currents*, **4**: e4facf9d99b997, 2012. doi: 10.1371/4facf9d99b997.

[49] Nishizawa, M., Hoshide, S., Shimpo, M. & Kario, K., Disaster hypertension: experience from the great East Japan earthquake of 2011. *Current Hypertension Reports*, **14(5)**, pp. 375–381, 2012.

[50] Ueda, S., Hanzawa, K., Shibata, M. & Suzuki, S., High prevalence of deep vein thrombosis in tsunami-flooded shelters established after the great East-Japan earthquake. *Tohoku Journal of Experimental Medicine*, **227(3)**, pp. 199–202, 2012.

[51] Kanno, T., Iijima, K., Abe, Y., Koike, T., Shimada, N., Hoshi, T., Sano, N., Ohyauchi, M., Ito, H., Atsumi, T., Konishi, H., Asonuma, S. & Shimosegawa, T., Peptic ulcers after the Great East Japan earthquake and tsunami: possible existence of psychosocial stress ulcers in humans. *Journal of Gastroenterology*. 2012 Oct 3. [Epub ahead of print].

[52] WHO. *Psychosocial Consequences of Disasters: Prevention and Management*. WHO/MNH/PSF/91.3. 1992. World Health Organization: Geneva, Switzerland.

[53] Norris, F., Friedman, M., Watson, P., Byrne, C., Diaz, E. & Kaniasty, K., 60,000 disaster victims speak: Part I. An empirical review of the empirical literature, 1981-2001. *Psychiatry*, **65**, pp. 207–239, 2002.

[54] van Griensven, F., Chakkraband, M.L., Thienkrua, W., Pengjuntr, W., Lopes Cardozo, B., Tantipiwatanaskul, P., Mock, P.A., Ekassawin, S., Varangrat, A., Gotway, C., Sabin, M. & Tappero, J.W.; Thailand Post-Tsunami Mental Health Study Group, Mental health problems among adults in tsunami affected areas in southern Thailand. *JAMA*, **296**, pp. 537–548, 2006.

[55] Thienkrua, W., Lopes-Cardozo, B. & Chakkraban, M., Symptoms of post-dramatic stress disorder and depression among children in tsunami affected areas in southern Thailand. *JAMA*, **296**, pp. 549–559, 2006.

[56] Schultz, J., Russell, J. & Espinel, Z., Epidemiology of tropical cyclones. *Epidemiologic Reviews*, **27**, pp. 21–35, 2005.

[57] Kotozaki, Y. & Kawashima, R. Effects of the Higashi-Nihon earthquake: posttraumatic stress, psychological changes, and cortisol levels of survivors. *PLoS One*, **7(4)**, e34612, 2012.

[58] Rubin, G.J., Amlôt, R., Wessely, S. & Greenberg, N., Anxiety, distress and anger among British nationals in Japan following the Fukushima nuclear accident. *British Journal of Psychiatry*, **201**, pp. 400–407, 2012.

[59] Wilson, T., Chang, A. & Berro, A. US Screening of International Travelers for Radioactive Contamination After the Japanese Nuclear Plant Disaster in March 2011. *Disaster Medicine and Public Health Preparedness*, **6(3)**, pp. 291–296, 2012.

Flood Early Warning Systems

Knowledge and Tools for their Critical Assessment

D. MOLINARI, S. MOLINI and *F. BALLIO*, *Politecnico di Milano, Italy*

This book presents the results of an ambitious research activity designed to understand why Early Warning Systems (EWSs) fail. However, from the beginning, the objective of the research proved to be challenging: for two reasons. First, as yet there is not a shared understanding of what an EWS is among either research or practitioner communities. Second, as a consequence, it is equally unclear when an EWS can be considered successful or not. Because of this, the research needed first to define EWS and identify its components, functions, peculiarities, and weak points. Only at that point was a first attempt to evaluate EWSs performance possible.

The book is designed for a wide audience. The book can serve as a sort of manual for EWSs designers, managers, and users, but also has appeal for general readers with an interest in the subject. While the focus of the book is flood risk in mountain regions, most of the results can be applied to other hazards as well.

Traditionally early warning systems (EWSs) have been identified with monitoring and forecasting systems and their assessment has therefore focused only on the accuracy of predictions. The authors propose a shift in thinking towards the more comprehensive concept of total warning systems, where monitoring and forecasting systems are coupled with risk assessment, emergency management and communication aspects. In line with this, a new approach to assess EWSs is proposed that is based on system's capacity of reducing expected damages, with the hope that improved EWSs will result.

ISBN: 978-1-84564-688-2   eISBN: 978-1-84564-689-9
Forthcoming 2013 / 300pp / £129.00

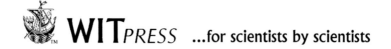

WITPRESS ...for scientists by scientists

Critical Infrastructure Security
Assessment, Prevention, Detection, Response
Edited by: F. FLAMMINI, Italy

Critical Infrastructure Security: Assessment, Prevention, Detection, Response provides the most comprehensive survey yet of state-of-the-art techniques for the security of critical infrastructures (CI). It addresses both logical and physical aspects of security from an engineering point of view, and considers both theoretical aspects and practical applications for each topic. The book emphasises model-based holistic evaluation approaches as well as emerging protection technologies, including smart surveillance through networks of intelligent sensing devices.

   Chapters investigate recently developed methodologies and tools for CI analysis as well as strategies and technologies for CI protection in the following strongly interrelated and multidisciplinary main fields: Vulnerability analysis and risk assessment; Threat prevention, detection and response; Emergency planning and management. Chapters are written by experts in the field, invited by the editors to contribute to the book. Researchers who participated are based at such institutions as Naval Postgraduate School, Argonne National Laboratory, Johns Hopkins University Applied Physics Laboratory, Pennsylvania State University, the University of Wisconsin, and SAIC.

   The book can serve as a self-contained reference handbook for both practitioners and researchers or even as a textbook for master/doctoral degree students in engineering or related disciplines.

ISBN: 978-1-84564-562-5   eISBN: 978-1-84564-563-2
Published 2012 / 326pp / £132.00

Landslides

Edited by: S. MAMBRETTI, Politecnico Di Milano, Italy

This volume is the second in the new Safety and Security Engineering series that is designed to provide a comprehensive view on risk mitigation. The book is devoted to landslides and debris flow, addressing the need for a better understanding of these increasingly frequent phenomena. With better understanding comes a greater ability to manage the attendant risk.

Landslides contains selected research papers presented at Wessex Institute of Technology Conferences. The Authors have revised their papers to bring them up to date and to integrate them into a coherent volume on the topic. The book includes the following chapters: Ranging scales in spatial landslide hazard and risk analysis; From national landslide database to national hazard assessment; An aid in the most accurate rainfall thresholds evaluation; Computer analysis of slope failure and landslide processes caused by water; The management of territorial risks: which integration between planning instruments, evaluation tools, and certification procedures; Analysis of the stability of slopes reinforced by roots; Experience with treatment of road structure landslides by innovative methods of deep drainage; Strategic program for landslide disaster risk reduction: a lesson learned from Central Java, Indonesia; Erosion of forestry land: causes and rehabilitation; Landslide in a catchment area of a torrent and the consequences for the technical mitigation concept; Slope instability along some sectors of the road to La Bufadora.

The book will be a valuable reference for professionals, scientists, and managers concerned with prediction and management of the risk of landslides and debris flows.

Series: Safety & Security Engineering
ISBN: 978-1-84564-650-9   eISBN: 978-1-84564-651-6
Published 2012 / 144pp / £65.00

Lightning Source UK Ltd.
Milton Keynes UK
UKOW032251130513

210591UK00001B/20/P